EARLY BIRDS

EARLY BIRDS

*An informal account
of the beginnings of aviation*

JOHN HALPERN

E. P. DUTTON   NEW YORK

First published, 1981,
in the United States by E.P. Dutton, a division of
Elsevier-Dutton Publishing Co., Inc., New York.

For information contact:
Elsevier-Dutton Publishing Co., Inc.,
2 Park Avenue, New York, N.Y. 10016

Library of Congress Catalog Card Number: 79-53334

Printed and bound by
South China Printing Co. Hong Kong.

ISBN: 0-525-93134-1

Published simultaneously in Canada by
Clarke, Irwin & Company Limited,
Toronto and Vancouver

Designed by Mary Gale Moyes

10 9 8 7 6 5 4 3 2 1

First Edition

EARLY BIRDS

EARLY BIRDS

"Crazy fools, the lot of them!"—that's how one old birdman described those daring young men in their flying machines. He then added, "They were the bravest and finest fellows I ever knew."

No more eloquent testimony to his observation can be imagined than the saga of Calbraith Perry Rodgers and the Wright *EX Vin Fiz*. Considering the fact that Cal Rodgers was the grandson of Oliver Hazard Perry, hero of the Battle of Lake Erie, and the grandnephew of Matthew Calbraith Perry, who opened Japan to the outside world, it is hardly surprising that he was determined to maintain the family tradition of derring-do. His distinguished ancestors having made their marks on the *water*, he opted for the *air*.

A publicity-minded newspaper tycoon and another corporate giant gave Rodgers the golden opportunity to exercise that option. The year was 1911, and the tycoon—William Randolph Hearst—announced, with his usual flamboyance, that he was offering a prize of fifty thousand dollars to the first intrepid airman who succeeded in flying across the country in thirty days or less. Cal Rodgers gladly accepted the challenge, and he proved beyond any doubt that although he may not have been the world's greatest airman, he was one helluva salesman and promoter.

His first step was to take a five thousand dollar gamble. He bought a Wright EX biplane, a contraption of spruce, cloth, and wire that bore a close resemblance to a very large box kite. Powered by a thirty-five-horsepower four-cylinder Wright engine, the plane—at the time a marvel—was capable of staying aloft for three and a half hours on one tank of gas.

Step number two. The handsome, cigar-smoking former footballer, exuding the bravado of a swashbuckler, approached the Armour meat-packing company with a grand idea. Should they agree to finance and sponsor his fantastic project, he would emblazon the wings of his plane with striking grape-colored lettering spelling out the words *VIN FIZ*. What is more, he would name the new Argo the Wright *EX Vin Fiz*.

Why Vin Fiz? Vin Fiz was a grape-flavored soft drink that Armour had recently introduced on the market. What is known in advertising circles as a "heavy budget" was earmarked for a campaign designed to ensure Vin Fiz's supplanting Coca-Cola and Hire's Root Beer in the hearts, minds, and palates of the American public. Rodgers's proposal couldn't have been presented at a better time. Think of the publicity, the prestige, the product association! An agreement was happily reached, and Project Wright *EX Vin Fiz* got underway.

The agreement specified that Cal Rodgers was to receive five dollars for every air mile flown plus the use of a specially chartered train that would follow his flight path across the country. Aboard the train were to be his wife, his mother, a crew of mechanics, a covey of Armour executives, and lots and lots of spare parts. In actuality, the Wright *EX Vin Fiz* would be following the train—not vice versa—as Rodgers intended to use the railroad tracks wending westward as his primary source of navigation. His fragile plane carried no instruments, with one primitive exception—a piece of string attached to the front cross brace. Whither it waved indicated whether the craft was going up, down, or sideways.

On the morning of September 17, 1911, Calbraith Perry Rodgers took off from Sheepshead Bay, Long Island, destination California and glory. A rather poignant photograph, taken just as he was a few feet off the ground, shows a group of twenty-five or so well-dressed well-wishers waving their derbies and fedoras to say "Bon Voyage." Would that they had known!

That first day's flight went quite well. Evening brought him to Middletown, New York, where he landed in a pasture. The next day's flight was not so good. No sooner was he airborne than he crashed into a tree. This event proved to be par for the rest of his voyage. If he wasn't crashing into chicken coops or being battered by winds and electrical storms, something malfunctioned in the plane. Once he lost his way because he followed the wrong railroad tracks.

Thirty days after takeoff found him somewhere in the middle of Oklahoma. Although he had lost the fifty thousand dollar prize, he lost none of his deter-

The Wright *EX Vin Fiz:* Cal Rodgers's triumph and folly. (National Air and Space Museum, Washington, D.C.)

mination to be the first to fly coast to coast. His backers agreed, and the train chugged on below, as the plane—one forced landing after the other—flew above.

The fantastic voyage reached a happy conclusion when, on November 5, 1911, the Wright *EX Vin Fiz* touched down on California soil at Pasadena. Our smiling, gallant Don Quixote of the skies, one leg in a cast, waved a crutch to a cheering crowd as he emerged from his flimsy, treacherous craft.

His circuitous route had carried him a distance of 4,321 miles, with a total flying time of eighty-two hours two minutes, and an average speed of fifty-two miles per hour. His actual time from start to finish was forty-nine days: nineteen days over his original estimated time of arrival.

Even if by some miracle Cal *had* landed on time, Hearst, had he wanted to be chintzy about the matter, could have withheld the prize on the basis of a technicality. The fifty thousand dollars were to be awarded to the first person who flew the *same* plane from coast to coast, and by no stretch of the imagination could this have been claimed for the plane that landed in Pasadena, which ended up far different from the one that took off from Sheepshead Bay. Largely because of sixty-five forced landings—most of them at least as painful to the body as to the spirit —all that was left of the original plane were its vertical rudder and drip pan. One estimate stated that four planes could have been assembled from the replacement parts alone.

It was a small matter that Cal Rodgers crashed as much as flew his way across the United States; his was a remarkable feat of courage, endurance, and determination. He failed to win the prize, but beyond question he earned an honored place among those "bravest and finest fellows."

Now for his place among that bunch of "crazy fools." In recognition of his great achievement, the Aero Club of America awarded him its gold medal. That, plus newfound fame and adulation, certainly seems to have gone to his head. How else to explain what ensued? He decided to become a stunt pilot. In those days stunt flying was a game of Russian roulette played with a gun whose every other chamber was loaded. Cal, somewhat addled by his new glamour, gaily played this madman's game for five months; then he lost. Flying low along the San Diego coastline, he attempted a to-hell-with-it-all act of aeronautical bravado that would give his admiring audience below the thrill of their lives. It proved to be his last thrill, when his plane gave a sudden dip, crashing into the surf. Calbraith Perry Rodgers was no more.

Such was the cockamamie state of aviation in the year 1911. Emerging triumphant on crutches at the conclusion of some aeronautical tour de force was at least as much the rule as the exception.

Those who emerged in any shape at all were the lucky ones. Not for nothing were the flimsy contrivances they piloted nicknamed "flying coffins." These improbable concoctions of cloth, bamboo, piano wire, and glue were kept precariously aloft by underpowered, undependable engines that were prone to conk out at such critical times as takeoffs and landings. Totally lacking any guidance instrumentation or any proper wing-surface control, the planes were totally at the mercy of the elements.

Why, then, would anybody in his right mind have dared set foot in such a device? The answer will never be given more poetically than in these words written in 1910 by Ralph Johnstone just three days before he fell to his death:

> It's going to get me some day. It's sooner or later going to get us all. Don't think our aim is the advancement of science. That is secondary and is worked out by the men on the ground. When you get into the air, you get the intoxication of flying. No man can help feeling it. Then he begins to flirt with it, tilt his plane into all sorts of dangerous angles, dips and circles. This feeling is only the trap it sets for us. (Vecsey and Dade, *Getting Off the Ground*, p. 4)

With the exception of a few fanatically dedicated souls, including the Wright brothers and their arch-rival Glenn Curtiss, the airplane was generally considered to be nothing more than an implement of a fascinating and dangerous sport called aviation.

Among those few who took the larger view was the then president of the United States, Theodore Roosevelt. He didn't need much convincing when, in the spring of 1907, a delegation from the Aero Club of America paid him a visit, the purpose of which was to sell him on the idea of the airplane as an instrument of war. Think of the potential—observation, bombing, strafing. Here was a "big stick" indeed. Bully!

Just seven months following this momentous conference, Signal Corps Specification No. 486 was issued providing for "the construction of a flying machine supported entirely by the dynamic reaction of the atmosphere and having no gas bag." The specification further required that the plane must reach a minimum speed of at least forty miles per hour, stay aloft no less than an hour, carry two persons weighing a total of no less than 350 pounds, be steerable in all directions and under control at all times. And last, but hardly least, the successful bidder had to "include the instruction of two men in the handling and operation of this machine." This was indeed a wise inclusion as no one in the army knew how to fly. In any event the builder, of necessity, would have had to be the instructor because different methods of flight control were utilized by various manufacturers. The joy stick and foot pedals—French contributions—had yet to be adopted as the standard means of piloting a plane.

Bids were solicited, and forty-one plane builders—among them the Wright brothers—eagerly responded. Their eagerness was soon tempered when, upon taking a hard second look, they realized what Specification No. 486 entailed. The Army Signal Corps was, in effect, settling for nothing less than a world-record breaker.

That "catch 22" left only the Wrights and two other bidders as qualified contenders. The other two (presumably having taken a hard *third* look at Specification No. 486) dropped out, thus giving the Wright brothers a victory through default. For Orville the victory proved to be Pyrrhic.

On September 10, 1908, a contract was signed, and the Wrights undertook the historic task of constructing Plane No. 1, United States Army. No sooner was the ink dry on the contract than these remarkable inventors got right to work. They had promised to produce a great plane in just under two hundred days—and they did.

A Wright Flyer, together with brother Orville, arrived at Fort Myer, Virginia, on August 20, 1908. Wilbur was in France, having sold a plane to the government and being treated like royalty. Both brothers were completely confident that their Flyer would meet or exceed the tough terms of Specification No. 486.

After some delays and much preparation, on September 9 Orville decided to "take 'er up." On the ground he had an audience of one—Augustus Post, secretary of the Aero Club of America. Orville informed Post that he would be aloft for only a short while, a routine checkout so to speak. Post, conscientious fellow that he was, clicked on his stopwatch just as the plane's wheels left the ground. It is well that he did, because, while minute piled upon minute, as he followed the sweep hand with increasing amazement, he realized that something besides Orville was in the air—a clear possibility that this "routine" checkout flight was about to break the world's endurance record. Hardly able to contain himself, Post peered into the sky and saw Orville descending to land. The instant his wheels touched ground Post clicked his stopwatch. Time? Fifty-seven minutes and thirty-one seconds, a world's record.

This fine beginning was soon followed by another signal event. Orville flew with a passenger, Lieutenant Frank P. Lahm, the first army officer to take part in an aviation exercise.

Hopes that were running higher and higher as several more successful flights followed were destroyed when tragedy struck. Orville, with another passenger aboard—Lieutenant Thomas E. Selfridge—had been in the air for only three or four minutes when, at an altitude of 125 feet, a crack in the propeller caused it to loosen and hit a guy wire. The Flyer took a sudden dive and crashed to the ground. Ironically, as a result of this accident, the army suffered its first aviation casualty even before it owned a plane, because Lieutenant Selfridge died just a few hours later. Orville lived, but he sustained terrible injuries.

This nattily dressed fellow would be well advised to put his right hand on the control wheel, because his Curtiss pedalless Pusher is one of the trickiest planes ever. (Silver Hill Museum, Silver Hill, Md.)

As to what happened afterward, it would appear that the army took a benign view of what can only be described as a tragic failure. Instead of dismissing the Wrights, the brothers were informed that they should proceed with further testing as soon as they could provide another plane. Cold reasoning, not charitable forgiveness, led the military to this decision. After all, the Flyer *did* perform beautifully, and as for the crash, well, it was just one of those unfortunate things. More important, there was nobody around both qualified and willing to undertake the task *except* the Wright brothers.

Despite the fact that Orville had spent seven painful months in the hospital, both he and Wilbur (recently returned from France) were on hand when a new and improved Flyer arrived at Fort Myer in June 1909.

On this second occasion things went off without a hitch. After only one month of test flying, the brothers informed the army that they were ready to proceed with the acceptance trials. Orville—his health regained and his confidence restored—would once again be at the controls.

July 27 was the date chosen to complete two of the requirements: endurance of at least one hour in the air and the ability to carry two persons with a combined weight of 350 pounds. Orville took off with his good friend Lieutenant Lahm and they stayed up for one hour, twelve minutes, and forty seconds—a new two-man flight world's record. Two down, two to go!

The two final trials, for speed and distance, took place just three days later. A crowd of 7,000 was on hand to cheer as Orville and his passenger, Lieutenant Benjamin D. Foulois—later to become a major general and Chief of Staff of the Army Air Corps—stepped aboard the Flyer. They took off and made a beeline for Shuter's Hill in Alexandria, Virginia, where a captive balloon served as a floating marker. They rounded the marker, beelined back, and completed the journey. This time three world's records were achieved for a two-man flight: average speed, forty-two and a half miles per hour; distance, ten miles; and altitude, 400 feet.

One more condition remained to be fulfilled, flight training for two army officers. Lieutenants Lahm and Foulois were originally selected to be the candidates, but Foulois, who had been sent on a mission to Paris, was replaced by Lieutenant Frederic E. Humphreys. Lahm and Humphreys, after a short but intensive period of training, earned their wings; the Wrights, having fulfilled all the conditions of their contract, received thirty thousand dollars and the army now possessed an air force consisting of one airplane.

What followed next was pure comic opera. No sooner had Lahm and Humphreys learned how to fly than they were reassigned to their former posts. The story became even more ludicrous. Lahm decided to take the Flyer up one last time. It came perilously close to being the last time for both pilot and plane when Lahm ended that phase of his career in a crash. Now the army's air force consisted of one badly damaged airplane and no fully trained pilot.

Lieutenant Foulois—recently returned from his Paris mission—had received three free flying lessons from the Wrights. With that experience under his belt, this fine officer found himself standing stiffly at attention before General James Allen, Chief Signal Officer of the Army, to receive his new orders. What happened is wonderfully told in Foulois's own words:

> "Don't worry," said Gen. James Allen, chief Army signal officer. "You'll learn those techniques as you go along. I've decided to send you and the flying machine to Texas. The weather is better there."
>
> "Very good, sir. Have you any special instructions?"
>
> "Your orders are simple, Lieutenant. You are to evaluate the airplane. Just take plenty of parts—and teach yourself to fly." (Glines, *The Compact History of the United States Air Force*, p. 56)

Foulois could hardly have been blamed had it occurred to him that he was merely another pawn in the old army game of posting an unpromising officer to an assignment that leads nowhere. Even more might this thought have hit him when he was informed of the allocation he was to receive—the first Air Force budget—for parts and one year's maintenance: one hundred and fifty dollars.

Because he *was* one, Foulois took it like a soldier. Reporting for duty at Fort Sam Houston, San Antonio, on February 5, 1910, he soon started a voluminous correspondence with Orville Wright, for reasons that are best expressed in his own words:

> Much of my time at San Antonio's storied Fort Sam Houston that spring was spent writing to Orville Wright, asking him how to execute basic maneuvers, how to avoid basic disasters—in short, how to fly an airplane. So far as I know, I am the only pilot in history to have learned to fly by correspondence. (Glines, *Compact History*, p. 56)

And there you have it—the bizarre beginning of the awesome United States Air Force: one banged-up airplane and one correspondence-course student flyer.

Foulois succeeded. With the aid of eight enlisted men and Orville's letters—he put the Flyer back together again, then flew it. Despite numerous crackups he kept at it until he became a first-rate pilot. At last the army could boast that it had an airplane that worked and an officer who could fly it.

Foulois's chief, General Allen, was so impressed that in the fall of 1910 he requested funds for the purchase of twenty additional planes. Symptomatic of the government's attitude toward aviation was this reaction from a congressman: "Why all this fuss about planes for the Army? I thought we had one."

The congressman was echoing an almost universal sentiment. America—the land that gave birth to the airplane—was fast losing its interest in aviation. The public still regarded it as a daredevil sport, but one beginning to lose the appeal of its first bloom, and the government saw no military advantage that justified any large expenditure.

Thus, in 1912 when the Secretary of War asked for an appropriation of two million dollars for the purchase of 120 planes, he was given one hundred and twenty-five thousand dollars and told to make do, at a time when the German government had allocated twenty million dollars to develop the airplane as an effective instrument of war.

Shortsightedness inevitably leads to long-term loss, and America's apathy regarding aviation proved to be no exception. Europe soon took the lead—both in numbers and quality of aircraft—a lead that we never really regained until World War II. In 1913, out of a total of 2,400 pilots in the world, only 50 were American.

Starting with Leonardo da Vinci, European interest in aeronautics grew progressively over the years. This interest culminated in a day that is indeed one to remember in the annals of historic flight. On November 21, 1783, two men—one a chemistry professor, Jean François Pilâtre de Rozier, the other an army major, the Marquis François Laurent d'Arlandes—became the world's first two aeronauts. Followed by the admiring gazes of Louis XVI and Marie Antoinette, they ascended in a Montgolfier hot-air balloon, remained aloft for twenty-five minutes, and traveled a distance of almost two miles. The Wright brothers and their moment of triumph at Kitty Hawk, North Carolina, were 120 years in the future.

By 1804, after perusing everything known about aerodynamics, Sir George Cayley not only had worked out most of the theoretical problems of flight but had built a five-foot model glider that flew. Thus, there are those (especially among the English) who consider him to be the real father of heavier-than-air flight.

In 1842 Cayley's compatriot, William Samuel

A remarkably accurate miniaturized model of the first man-carrying airborne vehicle: the Montgolfier hot-air balloon. (National Air and Space Museum, Washington, D.C.)

Henson, designed and patented a true man-carrying, powered, fixed-wing airplane, the specifications of which, especially for that time, were truly staggering. If one can believe the illustrations, the plane would have looked like an advanced model even as late as 1915. Its plans called for a wingspan of 150 feet (over three times the length of the original Wright Flyer), a fuselage-contained steam engine of twenty-five to thirty horsepower, and it was to be driven by two enormous pusher propellers—the first design application of propellers to fixed-wing aircraft in history.

What do the initials TWA, KLM, JAL, and SAS bring to mind? Airlines, of course! Anybody ever hear of ATC? Don't worry, it doesn't exist, but if matters had proceeded in a manner more favorable to William Henson's liking, ATC might well be included with those other illustrious airlines. Not only did this amazing man design the revolutionary Aerial Steam Carriage—as his plane was called—he planned at the same time to organize the world's first airline as its operator: the Aerial Transit Company. More's the pity that neither plane nor company got off the ground.

Throughout the rest of the century, Englishmen, Frenchmen, Germans, Italians, and Russians were building heavier-than-air craft by the carload: some of them outrageous, some promising. There is no question but that a few of these pre–Kitty Hawk efforts were on the right track. However, no matter what their degree of promise, they were stopped by a seemingly insuperable obstacle: inefficient engines.

That problem was taken care of once and for all when Gottlieb Daimler patented one of the first successful high-speed internal-combustion engines in 1885. Here at last was a source of motive power that gave great promise in terms of significantly reducing the weight to horsepower ratio that consistently plagued those early aircraft designers. It was Daimler's invention—vastly improved by the Wrights—as much as anything else that got their first Flyer off the ground.

When word of the Wrights' fantastic achievement was flashed to the Continent, the news was received

Here is the Wright Flyer No. 1. When Orville Wright kept it in the air for twelve seconds on December 17, 1903, at Kill Devil Hill, North Carolina, he became the first man in history to pilot a powered aircraft successfully. (National Air and Space Museum, Washington, D.C.)

ceived with even more enthusiasm there than here. Spurred on by this long-awaited breakthrough, it was back to the old drawing board for hundreds of flying enthusiasts from England to Italy. Thanks to the new knowledge gained from the Wrights' success, "flight fever" soon reached pandemic proportions throughout all of Europe.

The honor of being the first to take off from European soil in a plane of his own design went to an expatriate: the rich Brazilian boulevardier and sportsman Alberto Santos-Dumont. More sportsman than anything else, Senhor Santos-Dumont was—as

the younger generation might put it today—"into" aviation strictly for kicks. The dashing young Brazilian enjoyed every minute of the fame he had received as the result of his winning a one hundred fifty thousand franc prize for flying an airship of his design around the Eiffel Tower in 1901. Now that heavier-than-air flight was "in," he was determined to add this new aspect of aeronautics to his laurels with another first: the first successful powered airplane flight in Europe.

The plane he designed—the Santos-Dumont 14-bis —resembled nothing so much as a collection of six box kites, one stuck next to the other, to serve as the wings, with an additional box kite attached to the rear end of the fuselage for a tail. It looked ridiculous, but it flew: 23 feet on September 13, 1906; 197 feet on October 23; and 722 feet at an altitude of just under 20 feet on November 12. Not too impressive, but Santos-Dumont *did* get his "first."

It was a Frenchman, Louis Blériot, who really put Europe on the aeronautical map. At first glance, it would appear that Blériot was an unfortunate individual who had gone bonkers, suffering a severe personality change that transformed him into a flying-freak. Is there any better explanation for the actions of someone who, having made a fortune on an automobile headlight patent, proceeded to blow practically every last centime he owned in order to build experimental aircraft, cracked up time after time, and, as a result, was left a physical wreck? Yes, there is. Louis Blériot, far from being a nut, was a brilliant

A somewhat modified replica of Alberto Santos-Dumont's Demoiselle. The original, built in 1907, had a fuselage made of bamboo. (Rhinebeck Aerodrome, Rhinebeck, N.Y.)

innovator and hardheaded businessman who was willing to risk life, lucre, and limb for what he was certain would be the big payoff. Unlike the Brazilian glamour boy Santos-Dumont, he was in aviation as much for the money as the glory, which detracts not a single iota from the heroism of his achievement.

To borrow a timeworn cliché, "Just when things looked blackest . . . ," Blériot—dead broke and hobbling around on crutches—stared opportunity right in the face. The *London Daily Mail* announced that it was offering a prize of one thousand pounds to anyone brave enough to attempt a flight across the Channel and who succeeded in the effort. Louis Blériot responded to the challenge with the alacrity of an athlete in top condition: crutches be damned! To those who tried to dissuade him, pointing out that for all intents and purposes he was a cripple, he replied, "If I cannot walk, I'll show the world I can fly."

It's hard to put in words readily explainable how perfectly awful it is to fly the Blériot and what a great admiration I have for the pilots whose raw courage often outstripped their piloting skills and knowledge. Of the 120-odd flying hours I have spent in Blériots, I am sure no five minutes have gone by without adding a deepening color to that streak down my back. (Tallman, *Flying the Old Planes*, p. 26)

Thus did the late Frank Tallman—one of the greatest stunt pilots who ever lived and a fearless man who had flown practically everything with wings—describe in his gripping book, *Flying the Old Planes*, the hairy experience one might expect to undergo should he decide to take up a Blériot Model XI: the same plane in which Blériot was to attempt his cross-Channel flight.

During the predawn hours of July 25, 1909, a crew of mechanics and helpers wheeled a Blériot Model XI monoplane onto a grassy field near the village of Les Baraques, France. Out of the darkness a small figure emerged walking painfully and slowly on crutches toward the plane. With the aid of helping hands, he seated himself behind the controls, then placed his crutches beside him on the fuselage floor. He nodded, and a mechanic gave a sharp pull on the propeller; the tiny three-cylinder Anzani engine sputtered, coughed, and soon settled into a rhythmic purr. The plane started to move, first slowly, then faster and faster. Exactly at 4:41 A.M. its wheels left the ground, and Louis Blériot was on his way to England or oblivion.

Down below, a boat, loaded to the gunwales with reporters, observers, and Madame Blériot, proceeded at full speed across the Channel, following

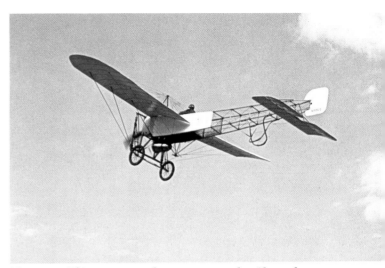

Not Louis Blériot winging his way across the Channel, but Cole Palen flying an original Blériot Model XI above his Rhinebeck Aerodrome. (Rhinebeck Aerodrome, Rhinebeck, N.Y.)

the direction of the plane's flight. Hoping, naturally, that the need might not arise, they were prepared to fish the indomitable Frenchman out of the water. What with the poor visibility, the choppy waters, and Blériot's physical disability, their chances of success would probably have been nil.

Above, unknown to Blériot, he had an unseen passenger aboard: Lady Luck. She more than earned her passage when sudden disaster seemed imminent. It would seem that the confounded Anzani engine (never noted for its dependability) began to overheat. A few minutes more of this, and it would conk out, driving the plane inevitably into the drink.

And here is where luck took over; it began to rain. Ordinarily the bane of pilots in those days, the downpour proved to be the blessing that would see Blériot through. Its cooling effect kept the engine humming, and before long the white cliffs of Dover came into view. Then, flying low over the beautiful green fields of England, he landed near Dover at Northfall Meadow. It was 5:17 A.M. when the plane touched ground. He had completed a flight of nearly twenty-four miles, almost all of it over water. In the by-now time-honored tradition he emerged triumphantly on crutches, waving one of them at the cheering crowd. Instant fame was his; great fortune was soon to follow.

Back home, almost immediately following his historic flight, Louis Blériot found himself inundated with orders for his Model XI monoplane from the French, British, and Italian governments. It was even necessary for him to found a flying school in order to teach his new customers how to operate their purchases. Beyond doubt, the Blériot Model XI was the

The pesky Anzani engine that gave Blériot such a hard time during the course of his cross-Channel flight. (Rhinebeck Aerodrome, Rhinebeck, N.Y.)

Pilot Palen brings the Blériot Model XI in for a perfect three-point landing. (Rhinebeck Aerodrome, Rhinebeck, N.Y.)

first production-line airplane ever to be built. Because of its comparatively simple construction, do-it-your-selfers all over the world were putting Blériot Model XIs together with whatever materials they had on hand. Thanks to local junkyards, mom's generosity in donating some of her sheets, and pictures of the original to go by, some pretty weird versions of Blériot's masterpiece were soon seen in the sky.

October 23, 1911, is an important day in the history of aviation. The Italo-Turkish war (1911–1912) was in full swing, when, on that day, Captain Carlo Piazza of the Italian Army flew a Blériot Model XI over enemy lines to observe troop movements: it was the first use of an airplane for military purposes in time of war.

In less than three years those four accursed Horsemen of the Apocalypse once again roamed the flaming skies of a stricken Europe. This time—wearing helmets and goggles—their steeds were planes.

It is hardly an exaggeration to state that the progress aviation had made in the scant eleven years following Orville Wright's first flight of 120 feet in twelve seconds was nothing short of astounding. Just look at the records that were established by 1914: speed, 126.75 miles per hour; endurance, twenty-four

hours; distance, 1,181 miles; altitude, 25,755 feet.

When Tommy, Pierre, Luigi, Ivan, and Fritz reported for mobilization in the fateful August of 1914, to say that the poor fellows didn't know what they were getting into is the ultimate understatement. Their rulers didn't, either.

The person who observed that war is much too serious a business for generals to handle knew whereof he spoke—especially if he had World War I in mind. In a mere matter of weeks following the outbreak of hostilities, it became horrifyingly clear who was running the war: the technocrats. The rapid-fire machine gun, the cannon capable of hurling immense explosive shells a distance of seventy-five miles, poison gas, the tank, the flame thrower: these goodies from hell, thanks to the technocrats, changed the face of war forever. Putting such weaponry into the hands of generals used to fighting other wars in other times was like putting a driver whose experience was confined to a horse and buggy behind the wheel of an Indianapolis 500 racing car.

Nineteenth-century tactics coupled with twentieth-century firepower inevitably led to the unprecedented carnage at Verdun, Passchendaele, Chemin des Dames, and the Somme. Shell-pocked fields, ravaged forests, burned-out towns and villages, drenched with the blood of millions, bore mute testimony to the fact that all the killing was to no avail. Neither side had gained a mile of ground worth the taking. Faced with annihilation if they continued as before and not knowing what alternative tactics to employ, both sides settled for stalemate, burrowing into trenches that extended from the Belgian to the Swiss borders.

The air war evolved in a completely different manner: from scratch, one might say. At the outbreak there were no planes available that were capable of combat. And there were no grand strategic plans, as there was no precedent to go by, for the obvious reason that aerial warfare was a brand-new game in the age-old arena of armed conflict.

When war came, the Germans, with their Rumplers and Taubes (Doves), and the French, with their Morane-Saulniers and Farmans, were equally matched, both in numbers of planes and trained military pilots. Each side had some 800 planes on a war-ready footing, their main purpose being observation, as no effective means of arming aircraft had yet been developed.

As for British air power, imagine, if you will, an air force of no more than fifty planes, barely in flying condition; a roster of pilots whose sole experience was flying "pour le sport"; and a commanding officer, Brigadier Sir David Henderson, who first learned to fly at the ripe old age of forty-nine.

These "flying playboys," as one newspaper dubbed them, would soon demonstrate with their bravery and daring how much more they were than that. One of their number, Lieutenant W. B. Rhodes-Moorehouse, was the first airman to win the Victoria Cross, Britain's highest military honor. All of them would prove, long before the Battle of Britain in 1940, "How much is owed by so many to so few." Of these few, not many would live to see the end of the war.

The first few weeks of war in the air had an unreal quality about them that bordered on the eerie. Pilots, perched high in serene and sunny skies, peered below to view, with horrified fascination, the nearest blazing approximation of Armageddon that man had yet achieved, all the while nary a shot had been fired in their direction.

Enemy pilots flying past each other on observation missions merely cast perfunctory glances at one another, although some ill-mannered fellows were so rude as to make threatening gestures.

No one knows the name of the angry young man who apparently thought to himself, "War, by God, is war, and I'm going to do something about it!" And he did, which made him the first man in history to engage in aerial combat: his weapons, two half bricks; his target, the nearest enemy airman's head. The idea took hold, and before long, stashing two half bricks in one's flight jacket prior to takeoff became SOP.

More ingenious dirty tricks followed, including dropping chain links on the engine cowling of a foe's plane in the hope that it would snag his propeller and force it to stop. Then there was what surely must have been the archetypal "mad Russian"—one Captain Kazakov—who was literally out to "hook a Hun." This flying Cossack had every intention of catching some poor enemy fish with the aid of a grappling hook attached to a length of cable.

The next step in this gunpowderless phase of the air war was an ugly one indeed. In the latter part of 1914, if an observer had been present at an Allied airfield, he would have noticed a cardboard box being placed in each plane prior to takeoff. Not box lunches, they were boxed death, because they were cram-full of nasty little steel things called fléchettes. Fléchettes—darts with razor-sharp fins—were designed with a twofold purpose in mind. Dumped on an enemy plane's wings, they were certain to rip them to shreds. They were equally certain, when aimed at the ground, to wreak havoc among those enemy soldiers unfortunate enough to be in the vicinity where they fell. It was claimed that one of these damnable devices would enter a soldier's head and exit from his crotch. In light of the far more lethal weapons soon to be employed, it is odd that not a single Allied airman would admit to dropping these revolting "pennies from heaven."

Some pilots, in their desperation to "get things moving," resorted to firing pistols, rifles, even shotguns at whatever enemy planes came within their line of sight, an act of aggression far more symbolic than effective. One observer, Penn Gaskell, in a two-seater plane went as far as to try hand-firing a Hotchkiss machine gun, a gesture that was not only futile but dangerous because the combined vibrations of the machine-gun firing and the engine more than sent his shots wildly askew; they very nearly propelled him right out of his cockpit. Proving the point once again, which every warrior since Xerxes's time has known to be true, never volunteer to do anything, the resourceful young airman received a sound chewing-out from his CO. The reason? According to this worthy, the machine gun's added weight not only slowed the plane down but also lessened its ability to gain altitude, thus hindering its primary mission of observation. He was probably right.

Even as late as March 1915 the airplane was not considered to be a fighting machine, even though it had proven its worth in reconnaissance during the first battles of the war, when English air observers reported German troop movements designed to cut off the English from their French allies. With that knowledge the British were able to devise tactics that forced a breakthrough, thereby preventing a consummate disaster: a World War I Dunkirk.

If planes were ever to realize their real killing potential, they would have to be armed with machine guns, and therein lay the real difficulty. The only effective place to position a machine gun on a plane was above the engine cowling, directly behind the propeller. With the gun in that location all a pilot had to do was point his plane in the enemy's direction then fire away. Technology being what it was at the time, had he done so, he would have become a kamikaze pilot forty years before anyone had heard the word. He might well have gotten his enemy bird, but he would have also shot his own propeller into smithereens.

The skies of Europe became frighteningly darker when the airplane was transformed, almost overnight, into a lethal killer. The biblical prophecy that men would be gnashing their teeth as they battled to the death in the sky came true with a vengeance beyond anyone's imagining.

It is a historical irony that many a prophecy has been fulfilled by an individual who would appear least likely to bring it to fruition. One of these was, most certainly, a young French airman who was to make terror in the skies a horrifying reality: Roland Garros.

Garros—the scion of a wealthy and well-placed family—was a dilettante to the manner born. Endowed with a charming personality, a facile gift of conversation that would have made him at one with

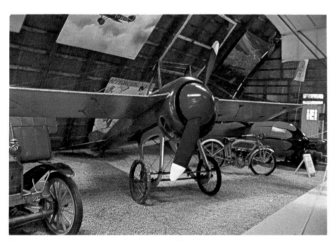

Deperdussin monocoque racer. Designed by Louis Berchereau in 1912, this streamlined beauty was the first plane to exceed a speed of 100 mph. Its sleek all-plywood fuselage gives it a most modern appearance. Deperdussins were flown by the French Air Service early in World War I. (Rhinebeck Aerodrome, Rhinebeck, N.Y.)

J. J. Mason of Los Angeles devoted eight years to the building of this beautiful Airco DH2 pusher plane replica. Despite the fact that it was armed with a machine gun, the original wasn't a very effective fighter because it was outdistanced and outmaneuvered by more advanced tractor-propelled fighter planes. (Mojave Airport, Mojave, Calif.)

the Guermantes, he was also blessed with what are known as "very good hands," making him a tinkerer nonpareil and a quite competent pianist.

The latter talent prompted his parents to send him to Paris for the furtherance of his musical training. Making certain that young Roland wouldn't feel lonely in the dazzling but impersonal "City of Light," they furnished him with a list of friends and acquaintances to look up, including Alberto Santos-Dumont.

No sooner was he ensconced in his quarters than he called on the celebrated Brazilian flyer. The impetuous young Frenchman informed Santos-Dumont that he had no intention of studying music; what he wanted to be was an aviator, and would Monsieur Alberto please make him one?

Apparently, Santos-Dumont was at first reluctant to become Garros's mentor; perhaps the young fellow's reputation as a dilettante preceded him. But then he noticed Roland's dexterous hands (just like my own!) and decided to give it a try.

Talk about "good trys"! This one proved to be one of the best ever. Roland Garros, a nice young man who showed no outstanding ability in anything, became, within the incredibly short space of a year, not merely a qualified aviator but one of the world's finest.

What that boy couldn't do with the flimsy contraptions that passed for planes in those days simply couldn't be done. He placed third in the famed 1910 Statue of Liberty Race only because the Paulhan biplane he had been given was unable to make a tight turn around the First Lady of New York Harbor. But from there on in, he was the best: in 1911, the one hundred thousand dollar Paris-Rome race, the Paris-Madrid race, the Grand Prix d'Anjou. Whew!

No one knows exactly how the publicity-hungry Santos-Dumont felt about the breathtaking results of his teaching. One can, however, hazard a guess that he must have felt *some* twinge of envy, for his pupil, in a single year, had become the indisputable master.

More than that, Roland Garros became a renowned mentor himself. He obviously enjoyed his fame (which amounted to adulation throughout Europe), but his interest in flying took on a far deeper meaning. Garros, as much as anyone, believed in the airplane's potential as the ultimate instrument of war. Cashing in on his newfound fame, he proceeded to announce his beliefs and concepts before the audiences of hundreds of the most influential people on the Continent who attended the many sumptuous banquets given in his honor. But guess where he received the warmest hospitality, the highest honor, and the greatest interest in his role of aviator-as-militarist—Germany!

Roland Garros had his German audiences hanging onto the edges of their seats as he described, in vivid detail, exactly how the airplane would assume a major role in modern warfare. Had he continued in this vein, the generals of the Imperial German Air Service might well have serenaded him with "You Made Us What We Are Today." But that was not to be, as Monsieur Garros's sojourn in Germany was to be cut short with startling suddenness.

It was August 3, 1914, when Garros, enjoying a leisurely late afternoon stroll, began to notice a fast-rising air of excitement in the streets. Crowds were gathering and people rushed to the nearest kiosk, grabbing up newspapers with an almost ferocious avidity. He froze when he saw the one-word glaring headline: *KRIEG!* War!

Now an enemy, he was undoubtedly on the high command's "most wanted" list and almost certain to become an involuntary guest of "Das Vaterland" for the duration. Zut, alors! He *must* escape!

For the remainder of the afternoon, he kept as low a profile as possible—not an easy thing to do for someone so well known. When night fell, he walked a circuitous route in the direction of the exhibition field where his Morane-Saulnier monoplane was hangared. Fortunately, no guards were around; they had repaired to a nearby Bierstube to celebrate a war that was going to be a walkover victory for Germany, and done with by Christmas.

Garros crept silently into the hangar, pulled the plane out onto the field, gave a sharp tug on the propeller, and, even as the plane began to move, jumped into the cockpit. In a matter of minutes, having reached the proper altitude, he pointed his plane southward and high-tailed it through the night (a feat in itself at that time) to Switzerland. He made it.

He remained in Switzerland for only a few days, then he sped to his beloved France. No sooner was he home, than he joined up. He was sent to Saint-Cyr-l'École (the French West Point), where he received the required training in close-order drill, rifle handling, and military etiquette. Upon earning his epaulettes, he was posted to the French Air Service where he—perhaps the world's greatest flyer—was assigned the usual mundane task for which the airplane seemed eternally fated: observation.

Not content with dropping half bricks or fléchettes, Garros knew in his bones what the airplane was inevitably meant to be: a lethal, flying gun platform. Put a machine gun on the engine cowling, point the plane's nose at the enemy, press the trigger, then—pouf!—one Boche less. Unfortunately, one Frenchman also less, as planes with shot-off propellers plummet to the ground. There *must* be a way!

He carefully examined the lightest machine gun available, a Hotchkiss, which fired 300 rounds per minute. Knowing the revolutions per minute of the

Le Rhône engine that powered his Morane-Saulnier, he calculated that, for every three bullets hitting the propeller, ninety-seven would pass through scot-free. Not bad, but not good enough, as a single bullet would blow the delicate wooden blade to kingdom come. Now, if there were only some way to *deflect* those three cantankerous bullets, then the other ninety-seven . . . Aha, that's it! *Deflect the bullets!*

With that inspiration Roland Garros would catapult the airplane into the forefront of all that was hideous in warfare. After some objections (It won't work. The deflector plates will loosen. Some bullets are bound to ricochet back toward the plane.) Garros persuaded the armorer to fashion two V-shaped steel deflector plates, which were then attached to the base of each propeller blade on his Morane-Saulnier. Garros's idea was that the configuration of the plates would cause any bullets striking them to ricochet at a forty-five-degree angle away from the plane. It worked, as we shall see, with devastating results.

On what has been called Bloody April Fool's Day—April 1, 1915—Roland Garros, true believer in the airplane's possibility of becoming the ultimate weapon, decided to show the Germans and the world the future. He climbed into the cockpit of his Morane-Saulnier—now armed with a Hotchkiss machine gun behind the propeller equipped with deflector plates—revved up the snarling Le Rhône rotary engine, then flew off to seek out the nearest airborne German. Together, they would make history.

That moment of destiny wasn't long in coming. In the air but a short while, Garros spotted an Albatros two-seater observation plane flying in his direction some 1,500 feet above. He immediately began to climb, not leveling out until he was 500 feet above the Albatros. Then, like a preying vulture, he stalked his unsuspecting victim, waiting for the moment when he could maneuver his plane into killing position: above and behind the enemy. All this time the German pilot and observer were watching Garros's seemingly pointless gyrations with mild but slightly perplexed interest. What in hell was this guy up to? Why didn't he just buzz off and do his job of observing their lines while they observed his? Live and let live.

As Garros made his final maneuver, the German observer, Franz Dietrichs, might have thought, *"Now* look at the silly ass. He's following us back to his own lines. Ach, those crazy Frenchmen!" If so, it was the last thought the unfortunate airman ever had, because Garros, in what was to become the classic method of attack, came in slightly higher and a couple of hundred feet behind the Albatros, his plane's nose pointed directly at it. He pulled the trigger, and his machine gun responded with a blazing fusillade of bullets that tore into both pilot and observer. He watched with grim satisfaction as the German plane plummeted earthward to its destruction.

During the next sixteen days Garros went on a one-man rampage that didn't end until he had downed five German planes, throwing the enemy into a state of near panic. After all, who wants to take part in a turkey shoot when he's the turkey?

Garros—already an idol in the eyes of his compatriots—was, more than ever, the man of the hour. On the very night following his fifth kill, he was inducted into the Legion of Honor. Mere mention of Garros's name automatically invoked the word *ace* —a Franglaisism of the time for anyone who was of championship caliber. Thus, he became the first air ace in history, and thereafter both sides dubbed pilots aces who shot down five or more planes.

The World War I German soldier sported—as part of his uniform—a large brass belt buckle bearing the inscription "Gott mit Uns": "God's on Our Side." If what happened next, vis-à-vis l'affaire Garros was any indication, the sentiment wasn't all *that* blatantly chauvinistic.

Because in those days every plane and pilot was expected to perform general duties, even the great Garros was sent on a bombing mission, the object of which was to drop four-pounders over the side on an enemy railroad siding. Approaching the target, he cut his engine so as to glide in slowly. He dropped his bombs. "Mission accomplished; now to start the engine." He turned on the ignition. "Merde! The salaud won't turn over!"

And so, Roland Garros, the scourge of the skies, frantically fiddling with his controls, sat helplessly in the cockpit of the same plane that managed to scare the daylights out of every German in the air, gently drifting lower and lower until he landed on a patch of grass right smack in the middle of enemy territory. He jumped out and did his damnedest to set the "secret weapon" on fire, but the wooden fuselage and cloth covering were simply too damp even to flicker. He looked up and saw a party of soldiers approaching. Before they saw him, he managed to hide himself in a water-filled bog. When night fell, he started to run for it—right into the arms of a German patrol. They happened to be hunting for firewood. "Ah, Herr Garros! So nice to see you again. We hope that *this* time your stay with us will be a long one."

It was. Roland Garros was a prisoner for almost three years. After numerous unsuccessful attempts, he effected a sensational escape, only to die in an air action a little over a month before the war ended.

Even as Garros spoke with his captors, his Morane-Saulnier's French markings were being replaced with the black cross that signified the Imperial German Air Service. The plane was then flown to Berlin where it was placed at the disposal of a young man whose sole directive from the high command was, "Make all of our planes as combat effective as this one."

The young man, Anthony Fokker, was the ultimate technocrat. He didn't give a damn who was fighting for what, his sole interest in the war was confined to producing the greatest number of the finest planes possible. A Dutch citizen, therefore officially a neutral, he peddled his wares to whoever would buy. In that spirit of strict neutrality he first offered his services to the Allies. Had they been wise enough to have accepted them, the war would probably have been shortened by months, because the thousands of planes turned out by his factory in Schwerin proved to be the backbone of the German air force, and marvels of their age.

Standing before his latest marvel, a Fokker Eindecker (monoplane), probably the best plane in the air at the time, he was handed a Parabellum machine gun (the first he ever handled in his life), ordered to mount it on the plane, and then add deflector plates to its propeller—"just like Garros's." Presumably, after suitable testing, all Eindeckers in the German air force would be so equipped.

Anthony Fokker listened politely to the request; then he made one of his own. He would like to be left alone with Garros's Morane-Saulnier. The German officers acquiesced, hinting that they'd certainly appreciate it if he would just get on with the job.

Fokker entered the hangar where the Morane-Saulnier was sequestered, stayed there for an hour, then, shortly after, informed the officers, "I have a better idea."

Fokker's brainchild was, in its simplicity, one of the classic examples of "Why didn't *I* think of that?" He merely fixed a cam ring to the propeller shaft, which actuated a lever. The lever, in turn, actuated a mechanism that pulled or released the machine gun's trigger, according to the propeller's arc: free air, pull; propeller before the barrel, release.

After a thorough testing of the prototype model, Fokker announced that he was ready to proceed with full-scale production. At that point representatives of the high command came up with *their* bright idea.

"Herr Fokker, we are indeed impressed with the results of your tests. However, before making a final decision, we should like to see the device tested in actual combat. Since you are best acquainted with it and are a first-class pilot yourself, we should like you to conduct that test."

Now it was time for Fokker's jaw to drop. They wanted him, a Dutchman, to go up and shoot down some helpless Frenchman or Englishman for whom he felt no enmity whatsoever. He protested, citing his

neutral status. They answered, citing his fat contracts. He tried one more tack. What if he, a civilian, were to be forced down behind Allied lines? He would be shot as a spy. "But you aren't a civilian, *Leutnant* Fokker!" With that he was given a handsome new uniform, complete with medals, and an ID card stating that he was Leutnant Anthony Herman Gerard Fokker of the Imperial German Air Service. "Welcome aboard, Leutnant!"

Right off, the reluctant lieutenant found himself up in the air seeking out the first Allied pigeon who might cross his gunsight. Air activity was unusually slight, so he had to wait two days before the opportunity arrived. But then, sure enough, he spotted a two-seater French Farman flying 2,000 feet below him near the Douai front. He steeled himself for the inevitable massacre that was to follow and made ready to dive. And that was as far as he got. Anthony Fokker—arch technocrat and pragmatist—simply could not bring himself to shoot down someone in cold blood.

He returned to the German airfield at Douai, reported to the commandant not only that he didn't carry out his orders—for reasons of conscience—but that he was prepared to abrogate every last contract and return to Amsterdam. The commandant, instead of having him shot for gross dereliction of duty and insubordination, replied sympathetically, "Ja, Leutnant Fokker, I understand." What he damned well understood was that you didn't kill a goose that was laying so many winged golden eggs—with more and better to come.

Leutnant Fokker, through the simple expedient of doffing his uniform, was once more Herr Fokker. At

Welcome aboard, *Leutnant* Fokker! (Rhinebeck Aerodrome, Rhinebeck, N.Y.)

the same time the high command brought in a pilot who was not only willing but eager to shoot down any and all of the enemy he might encounter. Leutnant Oswald Boelcke, a former schoolteacher, was most anxious to start racking up the record of kills that were to make him one of the war's leading aces before he, too, would be shot out of the sky.

After a few days of instruction in the intricacies of the gun mechanism, Boelcke was eager to go. On his third foray Boelcke got his bird and, upon landing, was able to report, "Mission accomplished, Herr General. The gun worked beautifully." A second Eindecker was fitted with the synchronization gear and handed over to another hotshot pilot, Max Immelmann. He, too, was delighted with his new toy. Additional Eindeckers, so equipped, were tried out by several more star-class flyers. They were all impressed with its murderous potential. By late August 1915 the device went into mass production, and Eindeckers by the dozens were throwing the fear of God into Allied airmen. The normally reticent English referred to them as "the scourge." For a time, there was no arguing the fact that the sky, from horizon to horizon, was German.

Then, in the autumn of 1915, the victory-starved French were most unexpectedly presented with one of the Eindecker planes. As did the unfortunate Garros, a German pilot landed his plane in enemy territory—but with a difference. At least Garros could console himself with the fact that his plane was out of control. Not this poor sucker. He deliberately, if unknowingly, set down on a French airfield, cut his engine and walked away from his plane, breathing a sigh of relief that he was home safe. Not until he heard the words, "Arretez! Monsieur, you are under arrest," did he realize that the field wasn't German. It would seem that he got lost in a dense fog, and, well, you know.

Blessed with this good fortune, it wasn't long before Allied aircraft, now equipped with the synchronization gear, corrected the balance. War in the sky became equally perilous for both sides.

The importance of the synchronized machine gun for air warfare cannot be overemphasized. Heavier, faster, more maneuverable fighter planes coming off the assembly lines soon gave new meaning to the word *deadly*. By the spring of 1916 French Spads, English Sopwiths, and German Albatroses, armed with double machine guns of unprecedented firepower, were raising havoc with what Eddy Rickenbacker, the American ace, called "the greatest sport of all": ground strafing. Whole fleets of planes zooming in a screaming dive from out of nowhere, spitting leaden death before them, mowed down terrorized soldiers who didn't stand a chance in hell of taking cover. Great sport!

The development of the true fighter plane heralded the age of special-purpose aircraft. The first war planes, outmoded relics by 1916, were assigned any task for which their limited capabilities were suited, such as dropping four-pound bombs or observation flights. The new breed had definitely prescribed roles.

As early as the middle of 1916 bombers by the hundreds were dropping fair-size bombs by the thousands on supply dumps, railroad marshaling yards, and airfields. But the "big guns" of the air really began to hit their stride in 1917. Two-engine night-flying Gotha bombers, beginning in May 1917, struck terror into the heart of everyone in London, as they dumped their bombs into the center of the city, an unwelcome visit that was to occur twenty-seven times during the rest of the year. Although Zeppelin raids had been conducted against London in 1915, their effect on morale was not nearly so bad, because the city's air defenses soon made such attempts unfeasible. With the Gothas, however, they *were* able to get through time and again, and, although the damage they did was comparatively not great, their effect on civilian morale was devastating. Paris, too, felt the thud of the Gotha's bombs. The blackout became a wartime way of life for both cities.

The air war was no longer the hit-or-miss improvisatory operation that characterized its early

These deadly synchronized twin machine guns were made possible by Anthony Fokker's simple synchronization gear. (Rhinebeck Aerodrome, Rhinebeck, N.Y.)

days. With a veritable flood of specialized machines —fighters, day and night bombers, observation, and photography planes—filling their arsenals, planners on both sides were developing tactics and strategies that were viable right through World War II. Fighter escorts for bombers and observation planes; the dropping of phosphorescent flares by lead bombers on night air raids, illuminating targets for waves of bombers to follow; "softening up" enemy ground troops with low-level strafing and bombing attacks before the start of an offensive. Sound familiar to you veterans of recent wars? Well, it all began in World War I.

Back in the late 1920s, an elementary school history class was asked by its teacher: "Who was the greatest ace of the war?" A flurry of hands would seem to indicate that the class was on sure ground regarding this one. The teacher pointed to a vigorously waving little girl, who piped up, with complete confidence, "Buddy Rodgers!"

For the benefit of those readers who were not yet born at the time the question was raised, it should be explained that Buddy Rodgers was the motion-picture idol of that hour. His latest triumph, *Wings* (1927), was the first—and for some, the best—of the Hollywood World War I air sagas.

Flashed in vivid color on the movie screen in front of them, audiences, rooted to their seats, saw the air war in all of its gory glory. Swarms of angry bullet-spitting planes locked in the mortal combat of a classic dogfight, others streaming the telltale black smoke of defeat as they plummeted in a screaming death dive, the final agony of the machine-gunned flyer, coughing blood, writhing in the flaming cockpit that would be his funeral pyre; it was all there and horrifyingly true to life.

No one who ever saw *Wings* ever forgot it—including the young lady who thought that its star, Buddy Rodgers, was a *real* ace. She may be forgiven her gaffe, if for no other reason than the fact that genuine aces were all but obliterated from public memory by the time she was old enough to go to school. America, then enjoying unprecedented prosperity and the frivolities of the Jazz Age, was in no mood to recall either a disillusioning war or its heroes.

How different it was when the "War to End All Wars" was in full swing! The aces were the sole authentic gallants that governments were able to offer a hero-hungry public. The Frenchman René Fonck had seventy-three kills; the Englishman Edward Mannock, seventy-three kills; the Canadian William Bishop, seventy-two kills; the German Manfred von Richthofen, eighty kills; these "Gods of the Sky," as the noted World War I air historian Arch Whitehouse

An RAF 2D coming in for the kill on a ground-strafing run. (Rhinebeck Aerodrome, Rhinebeck, N.Y.)

The earliest two-engine French bomber, a 1915 Caudron. The sliding glass windowpane beneath the bombardier's seat served as both a bombsight and a dropping mechanism. (Silver Hill Museum, Silver Hill, Md.)

described them, were a propagandist's dream come true.

They were the idols: not the poor miserable footsloggers, fighting an impersonal war, holed up in lice- and rat-ridden muddy trenches, emerging now and then only to face withering machine-gun fire, poison gas, and hellish artillery barrages. Where's the glamour in that?

Ah, but the aces! Like knights of yore, they

15

mounted their steeds (planes), readied their lances (machine guns), and bravely set forth to do battle with equally brave enemy flying knights. It's hard to believe in this iconoclastic age of the antihero, but the public on both sides regarded their leading aces as knights of the sky.

What was it like to be a member of this "superman's" club? Cast yourself in the role of a World War I ace, as we describe a day in your flying life.

You are awakened with a cheerful, "Mornin', sir. Time to get up!" It is still dark as your orderly helps you on with your heavy, leather flying togs. You go downstairs to the kitchen of the rambling old French farmhouse that serves as your billet and greet the other flyers in your squadron.

After a quick breakfast of steaming coffee, bacon, and eggs, you gather your men to deliver the day's briefing. "Gentlemen, a French ammo con-

voy is moving up to the front even as I speak. It's vital that it get to the poilus as soon as possible, because they're running short. Our job is to clear the sky of as many Jerries as we can. Just a few of their incendiary bullets could blow the entire convoy to smithereens."

You and your men walk out onto the field, now bathed in a rosy light as the sun starts to rise over the eastern horizon. As you approach your plane, its handlers wave a greeting. The chief mechanic grins, "She's ready for anything, major!" He's right. Your new Sopwith Camel—small, sleek, deadly, and beautiful—is the finest Allied plane in the air. You climb into the cockpit, put on your helmet, and adjust your goggles. You look to the airman with his hands on the propeller, and bark the order: "Contact!" He gives a sharp tug, and the propeller slowly, almost reluctantly, starts turning over. Then, spinning faster and

Almost before you realize it, your Sopwith is airborne. (Rhinebeck Aerodrome, Rhinebeck, N.Y.)

The classic V-shaped formation. (Rhinebeck Aerodrome, Rhinebeck, N.Y.)

faster, the blades rapidly fade from view as a diaphanous whirling circle appears, surrounding the plane's nose. A blue haze of exhaust gases envelops the plane, and the noxious odor of the hot castor-oil lubricant coursing through the Clerget rotary engine's innards fouls the clear morning air.

You can hear the deafening crescendo of your squadron's other planes revving up. Raising a gloved hand, you hold it high for a moment, then suddenly let it drop: Let's go! You pull the throttle back, and the rotary engine answers with an angry snarl that expands into a sustained roar as your wheels start rolling. Almost before you realize it, you're airborne.

You look over your shoulder to make certain the V-shaped formations that comprise your squadron are in proper place. They are, slightly above and behind. Turning your head to the right, then to the left, you see the other three squadrons joining up, which, with yours, will comprise the attack force.

In a matter of minutes you're flying at 5,000 feet. Still over Allied territory, you, the group commander, wigwag your wings; Follow me. You immediately pull the joystick back and go into a climb. Have to reach 15,000 feet before crossing over the lines into Jerry's domain. Don't want him hiding behind a cloud, diving down with guns blazing, while you, blinded by the rising sun's glare, are a sitting duck. You fervently hope the youngsters in the group remember the cardinal rule: Never engage an enemy who has the sun behind him. If you do, you're dead.

You've reached altitude, and a quick glance at your wristwatch and air-speed indicator tells you

that you're over enemy territory. You think to yourself, "Funny thing about Jerry; the blighter always insists on playing in his own backyard. Never wants to come over to our side of the street." [That is true. The Germans, with the exception of Werner Voss, always insisted on engaging Allied planes behind their own lines, a fact for which the American ace, Eddy Rickenbacker, held them in contempt.]

Peering below, you see a field of white mushrooming cloudlets; you've been spotted by the enemy. They're archies: explosive antiaircraft shells. You're not worried, because you're way beyond their range, but you know damn well that observation posts are alerting the nearest air base this very minute. It won't be long now.

And it isn't. Instinct alerts you to the fact that they'll soon be in sight. Placing a cupped hand over your eyes to relieve the glare, you anxiously

The alert having been sounded, this German pilot, his Fokker tri-wing revving up, can hardly wait to meet the Engländer head on. (Rhinebeck Aerodrome, Rhinebeck, N.Y.)

Watch it! Jerry may be lurking behind those clouds. (Rhinebeck Aerodrome, Rhinebeck, N.Y.)

peer into the distance, when suddenly—as if appearing from nowhere—you can make out what looks to be a large formation of birds headed in your direction. It's Jerry!

You wigwag your wings. At the same time, raising your right arm high, hand pointing downward, you move it back and forth. Dive! Dive!! Dive!!!

You calculated just right. No sooner is the fast-climbing enemy group flying 1,000 feet beneath yours, than you're in their midst, scattering their formation every which way under a blazing hail of incendiary bullets. Now it's every man for himself. Dog fight!

One of yours got one of theirs on that first attack. You catch a glimpse of the stricken Albatros D 3 going into a helpless tailspin, flames licking its engine cowling. Feeling the dread common to all flyers, you hope the enemy airman is already dead. Wouldn't wish the Götterdämmerungian end of being trapped while still alive in a burning plane on anyone.

As group commander and the most experienced pilot, you climb above the melee in order to gain a vantage point. You want to be in position to pounce on any enemy who's got one of your birds in his gunsight. And, sure enough, you

spot a Jerry coming in fast and behind an unsuspecting Sopwith seeking its own target. The Albatros is still out of firing range but, in a matter of seconds, he'll riddle the Sopwith to kingdom come, if he's not scared off. You bank to the right, then zoom in an arc that points your plane's nose directly at the enemy's top wings. You fire a short burst that etches a neat line of bullet holes straight across their diagonal. The pilot, frightened out of his wits, not knowing where the fusillade came from, goes into a sharp left bank, and skedaddles.

Quickly resuming your "mother hen" position above, you glance below to your left. You think to yourself, "Company!" as you discern—speeding like a bat out of hell—a distinctively yellow and green painted Fokker tri-wing coming straight at you. He's close enough that you catch the ugly grinning devil's face painted on his engine cowling's front. That means only one thing: he, like you, is an ace.

Seems their top flying boffins are allowed the privilege of decorating their planes any silly way they like. Can't say as you admire their taste, but you have to hand it to them, standing out like that: "Come try and get me," so to speak. This fellow is obviously the Jerry group commander and he just as obviously knows you're one, too. What's more, he knows your game, and he's determined to nip you in the bud. Well, let him try. It'll be a duel of your finest against their finest: both planes and pilots.

The engine cowling of this Fokker tri-wing replica, built by Jim Appleby, sports the same sinister face that Werner Voss, Germany's third-ranking ace, had on his plane. (Flabob Airport, Riverside, Calif.)

Company! A Fokker tri-wing heads straight toward its intended victim, a Sopwith Snipe. (Rhinebeck Aerodrome, Rhinebeck, N.Y.)

You'll get an arse full of lead, and that'll be that. (Rhinebeck Aerodrome, Rhinebeck, N.Y.)

A macabre contradance—your Sopwith does an inside loop. (Rhinebeck Aerodrome, Rhinebeck, N.Y.)

Still speeding in your direction, moments before he comes into range, he goes into an inside loop. The clever bastard will have you just where he wants you if he succeeds in coming out with his plane's nose pointing at your underbelly. You'll get an arse full of lead, and that'll be that.

But you join his maneuver, making it a macabre contradance, by doing an inside loop of your own. As you reach bottom and commence your climb, an inner voice shouts, "Press the trigger!" Everything happens too fast, but you do manage to see, with horrified fascination, a yellow underbelly being raked with incendiaries from tail to nose. It was all too easy. He came out of his loop before you were in his line of fire. You, however, were aimed directly at him when he was in the middle of his climb. A sudden blind-

ing flash of light deprives you of your eyesight, even as you feel the tremendous jolt that must surely tear your plane apart. Your body shuddering, you shake your head from side to side, blink your eyes, and focus down on bits and pieces of a plane and its pilot floating leisurely to the ground. As you begin to collect your senses, you realize what happened. You hit the Albatros's gas tank and it exploded. Thank God, your adversary never knew what hit him. You hope that, if the time should ever come when you "buy it," it'll be the same merchandise.

Fictionalized though the preceding scenario may be, it presents a fairly accurate picture of the touch-and-go existence faced by fighter pilots, day in and day out. Our "ace" is typical of the breed: intelligent, experienced, brave, cool under pressure, and possessing the mark of a champion in any adversary relationship: the uncanny ability to make the most of the slightest opportunity.

"To a much admired and honorable enemy.

From: British officers who are prisoners of war at Osnabrück." That is how the card attached to a floral wreath placed on the grave of the German ace, Oswald Boelcke, read. Hard to imagine, isn't it, in this post-Vietnam era, having such high personal regard for anyone who shot down forty of your fellows.

The fact is that aces, even on opposing sides, had a lot in common with each other. A psychological profile of leading aces, Allied and German, would reveal a remarkably similar pattern of shared personality traits. They tended to be loners, not outgoing or solicitous of their subordinates. In civilian life many of them excelled in such sports as horsemanship, car racing, and hunting; never anything involving team play or body contact. Valor and skill aside, there is no denying that the top aces were in business for themselves, fighting their own war in their own way. All of which led Sir Hugh (better known as "Boom," presumably because of his love of bombing) Trenchard, Chief of Air Staff, to state in 1917, "These aerial duels are a waste of time and manpower." As if that weren't enough, he continued, "It would be much simpler and more efficient to destroy the enemy's equipment long before it ever reaches a front-line hangar. One strategic bomber, a trained bomber crew, and the proper type of armament would do more in a week than all our multi-decorated aces can accomplish in a year" (Whitehouse, *The Years of the Sky Kings*, p. 186). How prophetic! Air war would soon become the mass-murder phenomenon of fighters and bombers working in concert as we know it today.

American volunteers had seen action in the Allied air forces almost from the start of the war, whether from idealism or an unabashed sense of adventure. Twenty of them became aces in the French Air Service and four in the Royal Flying Corps. The reason for the imbalance was the greater attraction the French, with their superior planes and training facilities, held in the beginning.

Then, in 1916, Sergeant Norman Prince, an American serving with the French Air Service, gathered together six other Americans, also on active duty with the French, to form the nucleus of an all-American escadrille (squadron). Their commanding officer would be French. By May 1917 they were in action, when they were joined by seven more Americans, including Raoul Lufbery. Lufbery, French-born but more recently a resident of Wallingford, Connecticut, was a mechanic working for a well-known French aviator, Marc Pourpe, when war broke out. They both joined up, and Lufbery went on to receive flight training. Later in the war—then Major Raoul Lufbery, United States Air Service—he would become America's third ranking ace (seventeen victories), only to die in battle.

Under their French commander's tutelage the squadron not only learned the ropes of aerial combat but they were soon weaving a few of their own, so well, in fact, that the German government voiced a loud protest to the American government. What's in

a name? Plenty, if a squadron fighting on the French side is called L'Escadrille Américaine, as was this one. *Américaine* certainly has something to do with Americans, nicht wahr? As if in tacit agreement, Prince and his buddies gallicized their designation to L'Escadrille Lafayette. Le Marquis de Lafayette—such a good friend of our country at the time of the American Revolution—would have been proud of his boys as they went on to achieve an honored place in the annals of air combat that is revered by patriots to this day. After America entered the war, they were absorbed by the rapidly burgeoning United States Air Service, where their hard-earned battle experience was to prove of inestimable value.

Ten years after the war ended Hugo Stinnes, a leading German industrialist, dolefully remarked to the author's father, "We never dreamed the Americans could deliver so much materiel and so many troops to the front in such a short time." He continued, "We were certain that we'd have won the war before a single American soldier ever set foot on French soil."

The battles of the Argonne, Belleau Wood, Château Thierry, and St. Mihiel, where raw young Americans fought with such determination, bravery, and zeal that the Germans were incredulous, dealt a severe blow to German expectations following

The alert airman manning the machine guns of this 1918 U.S. Navy Arenco observation plane *might* have seen combat, but not on this aircraft, as it never left our shores. (Movieland of the Air Museum, Orange County Airport, Calif.)

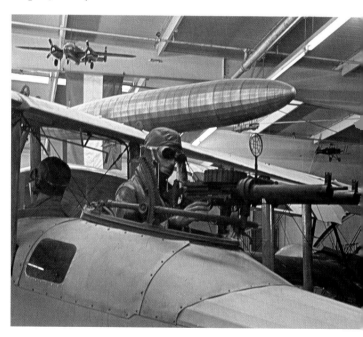

A Curtiss JN-4, or "Jenny," one of the several thousand that were built during the war. (Silver Hill Museum, Silver Hill, Md.)

America's declaration of war on April 6, 1917. It is indisputable that American soldiers and their weaponry were the decisive blow that finally broke the enemy's back. One grizzled German army sergeant grumbled years later about "our boys," "They weren't men; they were savage devils . . . all that gottverdammte Indian war whooping!"

As Will Rogers used to say, "From where I see it," from where anybody sees it, considering America's enormous industrial and engineering capacity, considering the fact that we were the very cradle of aviation, our war effort, insofar as the design and building of airplanes were concerned, could only be called a national disgrace. The sad fact is that not a single American-designed and -built fighter, bomber, or observation plane ever saw a moment of combat in European skies.

The only combat plane our aircraft industry was able to provide was an English-designed, two-seater day bomber, already outmoded, even as it was coming off American production lines: the De Havilland DH4—not affectionately known as the "flaming coffin," thanks to its propensity for unexpectedly catching on fire.

American plane builders could have followed the Allies' excellent advice and confined their manufacturing efforts to the latest English and French models, but they chose to ignore it. Instead, they built thousands of Curtiss JN-4s: the "Jenny" of postwar barnstorming fame. This crate, which had evolved from a 1915 design, was used solely as a training plane. Even in that role it was a second-rater. American boys who received their wings after eight weeks of flight training in these things had to undergo further instruction in modern Allied trainers before they were allowed anywhere near a combat-capable plane.

The end result of this irresponsible shortsightedness was that, when American airmen did go into action, they had to make do with foreign castoffs—mostly French. Despite that, our brave fellows covered themselves with undying glory, fighting against such superb planes as Albatros D 3s and Fokker D 7s.

What the Americans lacked in long years of combat experience and first-rate planes to fly, they more than made up for with their brash, enthusiastic "git up and go."

Thanks to organizational snafus, starting with General Pershing, Commander in Chief of the American Expeditionary Force, who wasn't all *that* impressed with airpower's potential—viewing it as nothing more than a supportive appendage to ground operations—American flyers didn't see action until April 1918. Our air effort really began rolling into high gear in August of that year, when newly promoted Brigadier General Billy Mitchell (who knew what airpower was all about and who would be court-martialed in 1925 for publicly telling it like it is) was placed in direct combat command. He molded his air force of 1,025 planes into a fighting machine that was qualitatively the equal of any in the world—a truly stupendous achievement.

A Nieuport 28 replica bearing the insignia of Eddy Rickenbacker's hat-in-the-ring 94th Pursuit Squadron. (Movieland of the Air Museum, Orange County Airport, Calif.)

In just seven months of active combat American aviators accounted for 781 enemy planes and 73 observation balloons at a cost to themselves of 289 planes and 48 balloons. In addition, they mounted 150 bombing attacks, dropping 308,000 pounds of bombs.

Pitted against the best the Germans could bring to bear, both pilots and planes, the United States Air Service succeeded in having eighty-eight aces among its flyers at war's end. Captain Eddy Rickenbacker—America's leading racing-car driver before our entry into the war—commander of the famous hat-in-the-ring 94th Pursuit Squadron, was number one with twenty-seven victories, followed by Frank Luke with nineteen victories, and number three was Raoul Lufbery with seventeen victories. Neither Luke nor Lufbery lived to enjoy the fruits of their victories, both, like so many others, having been shot down in their prime.

When, on April 1, 1918, the Royal Flying Corps and the Royal Naval Air Service were merged into a single organization—the Royal Air Force—with "Boom" Trenchard as its Chief of Air Staff, terror from the skies would soon achieve a new level of meaning.

Trenchard, a doughty veteran of the Boer War, who didn't receive his wings until he reached middle age, was a child before his time right up to the moment he was appointed to his new command. Heretofore, his peers had paid scant attention to his insistent idea that the military plane was essentially a tactical and strategic weapon possessing limitless possibilities, if put to proper use.

Now that he was sitting in the catbird seat, with full authority to do as he wished, he would show the world what air power was *really* all about! With that, he promptly formed the world's first strategic air force: The Independent Air Force.

This unprecedentedly powerful air armada, consisting of massive numbers of fighters and bombers, which worked as a self-contained unit, proceeded to wreak terrible destruction, not only among enemy troops at the front but right in the heart of Germany's industrial bastion: the Rhineland.

Trenchard reasoned, with the coldblooded objectivity common to all great warriors, that wave upon wave of large-scale raids, night and day, not only would reduce arms factories to rubble and keep great numbers of defending German planes from helping their beleaguered soldiers at the front but also would reduce the civilian population to a state of panic-stricken helplessness. He was right on all three counts. Air war had come of age.

November 1918: faced with two million fresh and well-equipped American troops joining the battle, with a revolution brewing in a homeland whose population, on the brink of starvation, was clamoring for peace at any price, the German high command capitulated, asking for an armistice. At 11:00 A.M., November 11, 1918, the war was over.

By war's end aeronautical engineering had made such tremendous strides that *breathtaking* would not be an inappropriate word to describe it. At the start 70-horsepower engines attached to flimsy fuselages, totally without armor, were hard put to achieve speeds of 70 miles per hour. By 1918 fighter planes, capable of performing the most intricate maneuvers, powered with 375-horsepower engines, flying at speeds of 154 miles per hour, and diving at 200 miles per hours—some equipped with as many as six machine guns—were a reality. Giant four-engine bombers, such as the Zeppelin RV-1, carrying a crew of eight in an enclosed cabin and armed with seven machine guns, were a portent of things to come.

Thanks to the god Mars, 177,000 military planes of all types were produced from 1914 to 1918, the last coming off the line having reached a performance level that would have taken a generation to equal had it not been for the needs of war.

When Johnny came marching home, he didn't come marching home to much. The same people who saw him off, cheering and singing "And we won't come back 'till it's over over there!," turned the other way when he complained of his new troubles. Imagine the gall—wanting his old job back—when the poor guy who took his place was having such a hard time making ends meet, what with the terrible inflation! The fact is that, because of the wartime economy's sudden halt as a direct result of the Armistice, unemployment was fast on the rise, and Johnny, the former hero, found himself to be Johnny-come-lately in the job market. It wouldn't be long before such treasured medals as the Distinguished Service Cross and Le Croix de Guerre were reduced to the proverbial dime a dozen in pawnshops all over the country.

The veterans who suffered the greatest culture shock upon returning to humdrum civilian life were the aviators—for a good reason. They *liked* what they did in the war. That "intoxication with flying," so eloquently expressed by Ralph Johnstone before he plunged to his death in 1910, never left them. For some, the psychological hangover that arose from facing up to the dull routine of an ordinary workaday world was too much to bear. Many of these former glory boys, unable to accept being grounded, fared badly. Others took a big gamble, knowing that the payoff was small, but it did give them the opportunity of doing what they loved most: flying. They became barnstormers. The author recalls a conversation years ago with an early bird who *was* a barnstormer:

I can say this—it was either fly or starve with me . . . and with a lot of other fellas, too. Hell, we didn't know anything *but* flying, and what's more, didn't want to. Don't you see, because we were all so young when we entered the service, hardly any of us had what you might call job experience. Flying was our life.

I took every last cent I could beg, borrow, or steal, and bought myself a war-surplus Jenny. She looked pretty bedraggled when I first laid eyes on her—but nothing that a new paint, varnish, and rust-removing job wouldn't fix up. And her OX-5 engine (a teakettle if there ever was one!) was in fair shape.

With my kid brother's help (he thought it was the greatest sight he'd ever seen), we painted the old crate's fuselage and wings sky blue with bright red ailerons and tail assembly. It was a pretty classy-looking job, if I do say so.

Even after the war, an airplane was an uncommon sight in many a small town around the country, so they'd be the ones you'd stick to. I'd fly low enough over a town to see people gawking up at my flashy plane; then I'd do a couple of loops to give 'em a thrill.

I would spot a grassy field on the edge of town and set down. You should see the look on the farmer's face as he came running . . . never saw a plane that close in his life! I'd shake his hand, give him a spiel about the wonders of flying, then offer to take him up. Some did; some didn't, but most of them were happy to let me use their fields, if only for the novelty of having a plane around.

After a while, people from the town would start streaming onto the field with their kids. Those kids! They thought I was really something, standing there in front of the plane, all decked out in flying togs with my goggles dangling 'round my neck. I'd lift one of 'em, show him the controls and let him push the stick; then I'd ask in a loud enough voice for everyone to hear, "Wouldn't *you* like to go up, sonny?" I can still hear the beseeching, "Pu*leeze,* Pop!"

At five dollars per ride, you did pretty good if you got ten takers. If you only got six, you barely broke even. It was no way to make a decent living, but being young, just so's we could fly, we were willing to put up with it.

One man's path to fame and fortune: the Jenny that Lindbergh flew as a young barnstormer. (Cradle of Aviation Museum, Mineola, N.Y.)

Despite these bleak prospects, barnstorming as a way of life took hold among a generation too young to have taken part in the war. For eight hundred dollars you could attend the Curtiss flying school on Long Island, where you not only learned how to fly, but to assemble planes as well. Would-be barnstormers, in their anxiety to hit the circuit, after only a few hours of flying time, were foolhardy enough to attempt those dangerous crowd-pleasing stunts that were the game's stock in trade. Such idiocy resulted in the school's losing seven pupils in a single week through crashes.

Commercial aviation was still in its infancy, and as there were more pilots than available jobs, barnstorming was the only solution to staying in the air. Some of America's most illustrious aviators followed this path as their first step along the road to fame and fortune, among them a tall, skinny, taciturn young fellow, known to friends as "Slim"; last name, Lindbergh.

"Never again!" became the ringing motto of both the American armed forces and the aviation industry as soon as the last shot was fired in the war. Concerted efforts, with government sponsorship, were undertaken to ensure that the United States would no longer be Europe's poor relation in the area of aircraft design and production. The effort paid off, and as the 1920s reached their end, American combat planes were considered to be the best in the world and her commercial aircraft equal to any.

However, before that goal was realized, American aviators were in the news once more with a world record. This time they were piloting a plane provided by Anthony Fokker.

The Army had bought two Fokker F-IV monoplanes: one to be used as an air ambulance, the other as a transport. Lieutenant Oakley G. Kelly, after test-piloting the transport plane (the T-2), came up with a bright idea. Why not fly it nonstop from coast to coast? Several unsuccessful attempts had been made, so if the Army Air Service could succeed, it would add quite a feather to its cap. Additionally, such a feat would prove the future feasibilty of long-distance, troop-carrying air transport.

Kelly's request to proceed with the project was answered, "Affirmative," whereupon he got right to work, modifying the T-2 to meet the demands of the grueling test it was about to undergo. Its fuel capacity was more than tripled, the center section of the wings was strengthened, and a set of auxiliary controls were installed in the cabin. About that cabin: sporting three oval-shaped windows extending from floor to ceiling on either side, painted in gold trim on the outside, this lumbering bird had a look that can only be described as *Victorian*.

It was decided to make the nonstop coast-to-coast attempt by flying a West-East course to take advantage of the prevailing winds. There was another very good reason for this decision; California refined gasoline (apparently available only locally) had a higher natural octane rating.

The Boeing F4-B, designed in 1928, was one of the best combat planes of its era. (Movieland of the Air Museum, Orange County Airport, Calif.)

Taking off from San Diego, Lieutenant Kelly and his copilot, Lieutenant John A. Macready, had flown no farther than fifty miles eastward, when heavy fog in the mountain passes forced them to turn back. Having nothing better to do, they stayed aloft long enough to set a world's unofficial endurance record.

Second go-round: this time it was a real heartbreaker. They got almost as far as Indianapolis, when a cracked water jacket caused the T-2's 410-horsepower Liberty engine to seize up, forcing them to land at Fort Benjamin Harrison, Indiana. That elusive feather was beginning to look pretty bedraggled, especially considering the brave words emblazoned in large letters on the fuselage's sides: Army Air Service Non Stop Coast to Coast.

Everybody knows the maxim, "Once burned, twice shy," but one wonders if a maxim exists for the *twice*-burned. If so, the team of Kelly and Macready paid it scant attention. Instead, they stuck with grim determination to the spirit of that old service saw, "The difficult we do immediately, the impossible takes a little longer."

Their third try was based on a different game plan. This time, still using California high-octane gasoline, they took off May 2, 1923, from Roosevelt (formerly Hazelhurst) Field, Long Island, flying an East-West course.

Hardly were they airborne, when the engine's voltage regulator acted up. In no mood to suffer the mortification of a *third* failure, Kelly took it apart right there in his open cockpit directly behind the churning Liberty engine, while Macready hunched over in the crowded cabin filled with fuel tanks, operated the auxiliary controls. Faced with the agonizing possibility of having to cancel the attempt once more, Kelly was inspired to get the thing working.

With that mishap taken care of, the improbable-looking plane droned steadily on through the rest of the day and night. Despite heavy overcast and rain that made navigation most uncertain, the two indomitable lieutenants finally sighted the landing strip and hangars of Rockwell Field in San Diego. Touching ground at 12:26 P.M., they had completed the nonstop cross-country flight in 26 hours, 50 minutes, and 38.4 seconds.

In 1924 one wouldn't have been expected to be impressed with a world-circling journey that took 175 days to complete, especially if by air. However, the Army Air Service wasn't particularly interested in setting any speed records when it sent a fleet of four Douglas two-place pontoon-equipped biplanes that had been especially designed for the flight on an around-the-world tour. As was the T-2 flight, its primary concern was promoting the airplane as a vital means of military transport, only this time the planes would be American-designed and -built and the dis-

Don't build them like they used to? Not so! "Frenchy" Sevard of Long Beach, California, builds exact replicas, with improved instrumentation and engines, of Ford Trimotors, which he sells to short-haul airlines that like them just fine. (Long Beach Airport, Long Beach, Calif.)

The most "moderne"-looking Northrop Alpha of 1930 was one of the last transport planes whose pilot flew in an open cockpit. (National Air and Space Museum, Washington, D.C.)

fuses) led to the Fords' buying Stout out in August 1925 and proceeding on their own.

Working in accordance with the organizational policies that made the name Ford synonymous with modern mass production, Henry and Edsel assigned a team of engineers to rescue the 3-AT project with but a single directive, which was, in effect, "Turn this turkey into a bird that flies." They did.

The initial fruit of their labors was the Ford Trimotor—the 4-AT—which made its maiden flight on June 11, 1926. It also made air transport history, because it was the first true precursor of the passenger plane as we know it today. Although its cabin was not pressurized, the wicker passenger seats were ample and comfortable, the wide windows provided an excellent view, and there were washroom and kitchen facilities aboard. It was a slow plane (cruising speed eighty-five miles per hour), but a safe one, being able to remain aloft on a single engine.

This plane and a later model—the 5-AT, introduced in 1928, powered by 420-horsepower Pratt & Whitney Wasp engines—became the backbone of air-

lines not only in the United States but in Canada, Mexico, Central and South America, Europe, Australia, and China: one hundred airlines in all.

By the early 1930s, with commercial aviation fast achieving the status of big business, flying was becoming less of an art and more of a science. Pilots who looked not to their instincts but to the complicated dials on their planes' instrument panels represented a new age's approach to aviation.

"When we put our helmets and goggles aside, dressed up in nice neat uniforms, and sat *inside* the plane, we lost the real joy of flying." These words, spoken so heartfeltly by a long-retired airlines pilot, tell the true story of aviation's early days. No matter the uncertainties, the discomforts, the dangers: those planes were thrilling to fly.

As for the early birdmen: just like old soldiers who never die but simply fade away, they *flew* away . . . in early birds.

They flew away—some in 1910 Hanriots. (Rhinebeck Aerodrome, Rhinebeck, N.Y.)

If the photographs of the beautiful planes that grace the remainder of this book give the reader the same pleasure in viewing them that the author/photographer felt as he took them, he will consider his efforts more than amply rewarded.

The photographic equipment used consisted of two Nikon FE camera bodies, a Nikon 50mm lens, a Nikon 35mm PC lens, a 28-85mm Tokina zoom lens, an 80-200mm Tokina zoom lens, and a Gitzo lightweight tripod. The pictures were taken with Kodachrome 64 and High Speed Ektachrome 400 film. A polarizing filter was employed for most of the outdoor shots, and a fluorescent light filter was used for those taken indoors.

Professor Samuel Pierpont Langley's Aerodrome No. 5 was
the first engine-powered heavier-than-air machine to fly.
On May 6, 1896, it was launched from a catapult, and
its steam engine drove it a distance of 3,300 feet in the
air. (National Air and Space Museum, Washington, D.C.)

The figure of Orville at the controls may be wax, but the
plane is the original Wright Flyer No. 1. (National Air
and Space Museum, Washington, D.C.)

BELOW

Cole Palen's Demoiselle ready for takeoff. (Rhinebeck
Aerodrome, Rhinebeck, N.Y.)

OPPOSITE TOP

The same Demoiselle high in the sky. (Rhinebeck
Aerodrome, Rhinebeck, N.Y.)

OPPOSITE BOTTOM

This closeup view of a Demoiselle shows the
far-from-comfortable seating arrangement for the pilot:
directly under the engine and behind the whirling
propeller blades. (Movieland of the Air Museum, Orange
County Airport, Calif.)

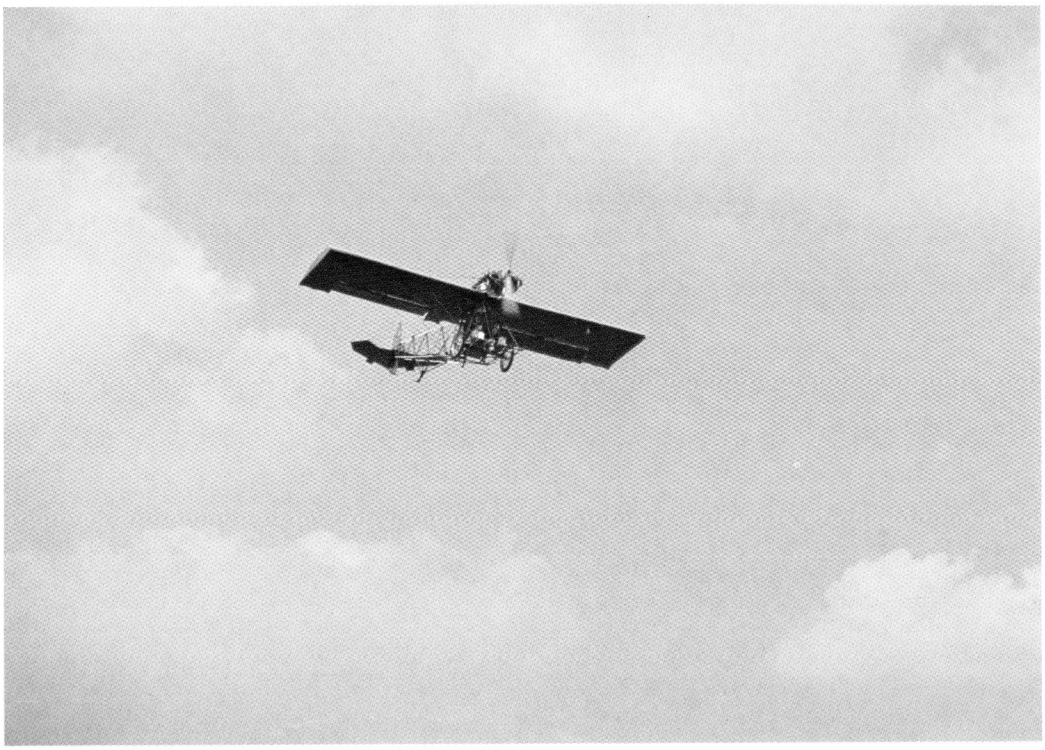

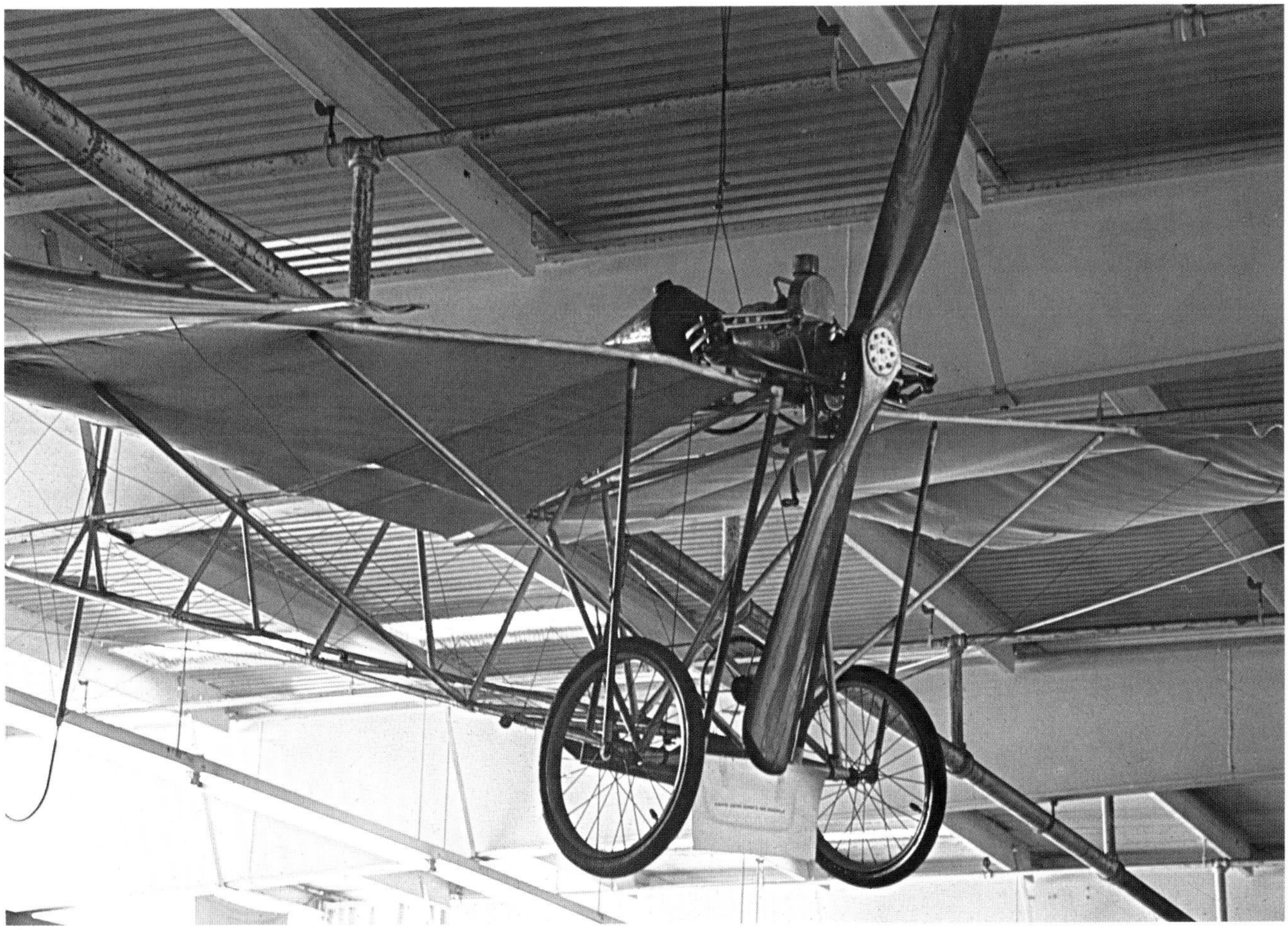

An original Blériot Model XI and a beautiful example of the superb workmanship that the reconstruction experts of the Smithsonian Institution's Silver Hill Museum are capable of. (Silver Hill Museum, Silver Hill, Md.)

An all-American Blériot? You bet! This 1911 model was built from parts supplied by the American Airplane Supply Co. of Hempstead, New York. (Rhinebeck Aerodrome, Rhinebeck, N.Y.)

How about a *Canadian* Blériot? Well, here we have one, built by students of the Calgary Institute. (Movieland of the Air Museum, Orange County Airport, Calif.)

An interior view of a Blériot Model XI, showing its fuel tank, controls, and pilot's seat. (Silver Hill Museum, Silver Hill, Md.)

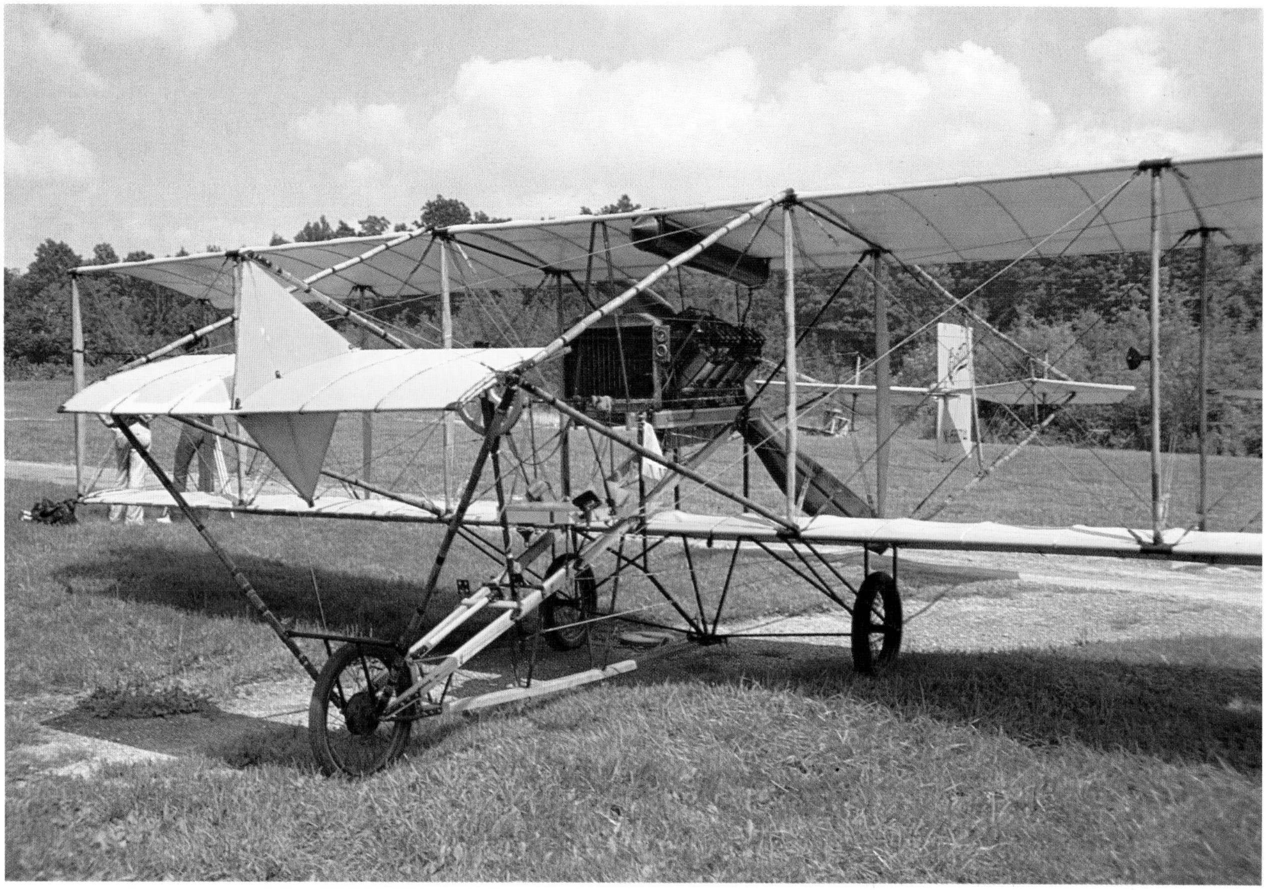

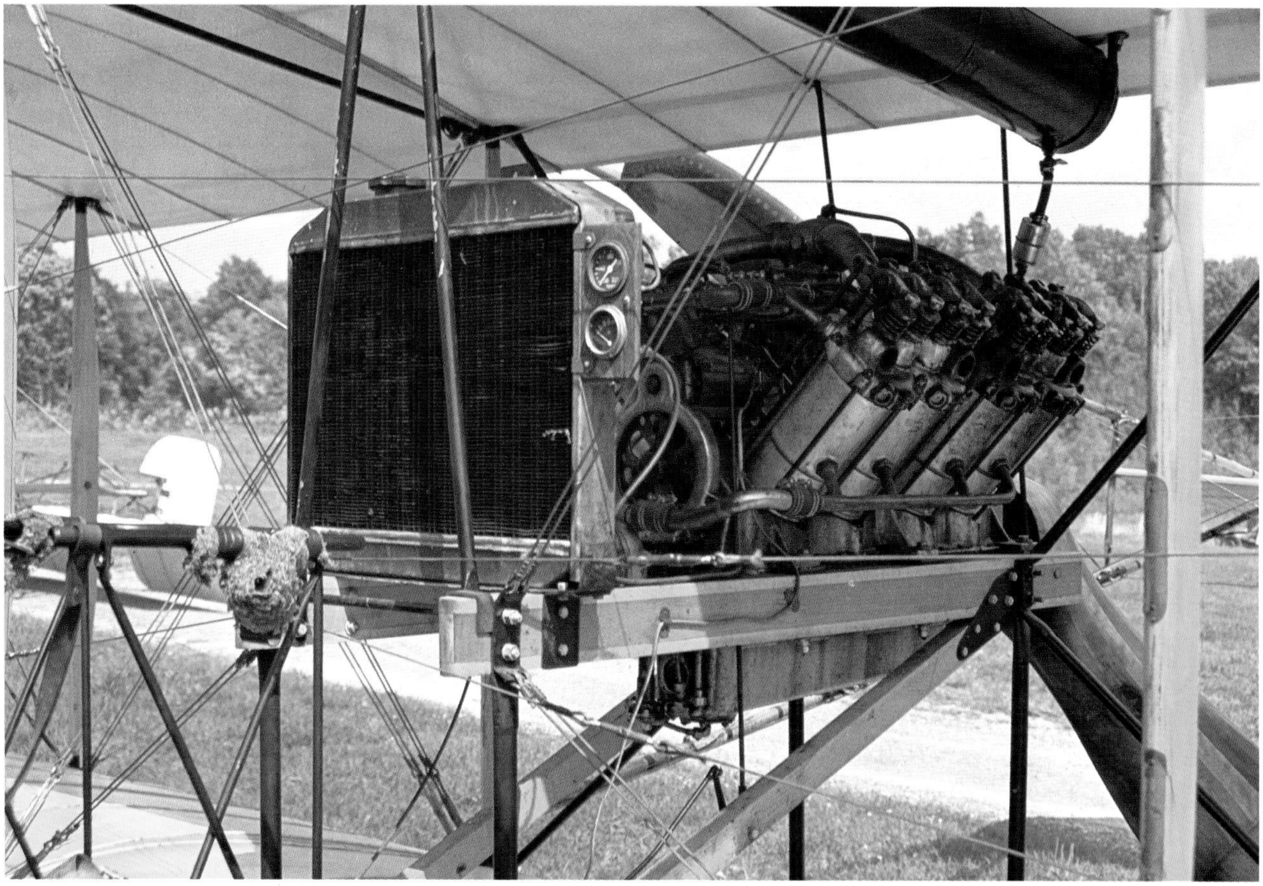

The 1911 Curtiss Model D shown here was a favorite of both the U.S. Army and Navy. (Rhinebeck Aerodrome, Rhinebeck, N.Y.)

Glenn Curtiss was as famous for his engine designs as his planes. Here we see the engine that powered his Model D. (Rhinebeck Aerodrome, Rhinebeck, N.Y.)

The Curtiss Model D is a feisty bird, but birdman Cole Palen knows, as he demonstrates here, just how to keep it in line. (Rhinebeck Aerodrome, Rhinebeck, N.Y.)

The engine is a 1939 Franklin, but the rest of this 1910 Hanriot replica is completely authentic. The Hanriot's fuselage was constructed using the same techniques employed in the building of racing skiffs. (Rhinebeck Aerodrome, Rhinebeck, N.Y.)

One thing about flying a Hanriot, you're certain to get
plenty of fresh air and sunshine. (Rhinebeck Aerodrome,
Rhinebeck, N.Y.)

Avro 504-K. This wonderful plane, originally designed in 1913, served as a fighter, a day and night bomber, an observation plane—you name it. When they became obsolete for combat purposes, they were used as civilian trainers through the 1930s. A total of 10,000 Avros were built. (Rhinebeck Aerodrome, Rhinebeck, N.Y.)

TOP

TOP

J. J. Mason's exquisite Airco DH2 replica, called the
Flying Kite. (Mojave Airport, Mojave, Calif.)

BOTTOM

"Leftenant" Mason, his mark. (Mojave Airport, Mojave,
Calif.)

The Smith Dolphin replica shown here represents 1,582 originals that were the first multigun fighters. When they appeared in 1915, they were greeted with some skepticism but soon proved their fighting effectiveness at altitudes up to 20,000 feet. (Rhinebeck Aerodrome, Rhinebeck, N.Y.)

Dick King's replica built from original drawings of a 1916 Sopwith Pup is powered by an original 80-hp Le Rhône rotary engine. Sopwith Pups proved to be more than a match for enemy planes that boasted twice their power. (Rhinebeck Aerodrome, Rhinebeck, N.Y.)

The Sopwith Camel holds the all-time record for enemy
planes shot down: 1,294. The prototype flew on December
22, 1916, the first of more than 5,450 Sopwith Camels to
fly in combat. The torque effect of its 130-hp Clerget
rotary engine made it an extremely sensitive plane to fly,
but in the hands of an experienced pilot, it was
unsurpassed in maneuverability. (Rhinebeck Aerodrome,
Rhinebeck, N.Y.)

A Sopwith fitted with a bomb rack drops a couple of
50-pounders. (Rhinebeck Aerodrome, Rhinebeck, N.Y.)

This elegant Sopwith Pup, built by Jim Appleby, is the
featured star in numerous air shows throughout the
country. (Flabob Airport, Riverside, Calif.)

The Sopwith Pup's armament consisted of a single machine
gun. (Flabob Airport, Riverside, Calif.)

The Nieuport 28 was more pleasing to the eye than effective as a fighting plane. Underpowered and structurally weak, few were ordered by the French Air Service. However, the Americans, who were desperate for combat planes, bought 297 of them. The Nieuport shown here is one of Jim Appleby's creations. (Flabob Airport, Riverside, Calif.)

It was largely in these Nieuport "castoffs" that American
flyers won their laurels. (Flabob Airport, Riverside, Calif.)

The Spad S 13 was one of the most formidable fighters of
World War I. Armed with two Vickers machine guns
and powered by a 235-hp Hispano-Suiza engine, it was
the favorite plane of such aces as René Fonck, Charles
Nungesser, Eddy Rickenbacker, and Frank Luke.
(Silver Hill Museum, Silver Hill, Md.)

Beautiful but fragile. The fuselage frame, made with
choice Sitka spruce, of a Nieuport 28 replica being
constructed in Jim Appleby's workshop. (Flabob Airport,
Riverside, Calif.)

This 1917 Morane-Saulnier, a parasol-winged, streamlined monoplane, was a most advanced-looking model for its time. Twelve hundred and ten of them were built for the French Air Service. The one shown here was standing on the field at Le Bourget when Lindbergh made his historic landing. (Rhinebeck Aerodrome, Rhinebeck, N.Y.)

The ungainly looking R.A.F. (Royal Aircraft Factory) SE 5a was perhaps the best Allied fighter plane of the war. Serving in twenty-four British, two American, and one Australian squadron, it was a favorite plane of the great RAF aces, Edward Mannock, William Bishop, and James McCudden, who achieved most of their victories flying R.A.F. SE 5as. The 1917 Wolseley Viper 200-hp engine gives the R.A.F. SE 5a its square-nosed appearance. (Movieland of the Air Museum, Orange County Airport, Calif.)

The Albatros D 3 was the reason British flyers referred to
April 1917 as "Bloody April." For a while it dominated
the skies, when it was flown by such German aces as
Manfred von Richthofen, Werner Voss, and Ernst Udet.
It was a superb high-altitude fighter but had a most
disconcerting tendency to lose one of its lower wings in a
tight maneuver. (National Air and Space Museum,
Washington, D.C.)

The Fokker Dr. 1 triplane was perhaps the most famous fighter of World War I, if for no other reason than that it was flown by 'The Red Baron," Manfred von Richthofen, and his Jagdgeschwader Nr. 1, "The Flying Circus."
It was in a Dr. 1 that von Richthofen met his end on April 21, 1918. Some 378 Dr. 1s were built but were obsoleted within a short time by the far more effective Fokker D-11. In the hands of a skilled pilot the Dr. 1 was an excellent combat craft, but woe to the others! It was one of the most dangerous planes of all to fly. The replica shown here was built by Cole Palen with most meticulous attention to authentic detailing. It is one of the featured performers at his Rhinebeck Aerodrome World War I show. (Rhinebeck Aerodrome, Rhinebeck, N.Y.)

The heavyset appearance of the Dr. 1 is lightened by the
gay orange and green coloring of Jim Appleby's replica.
(Flabob Airport, Riverside, Calif.)

The Fokker D 7 was so highly regarded that Article IV of the armistice agreement stipulated that every remaining D 7 in the Imperial German Air Force was to be turned over to the victors intact. When they first entered service in April 1918, they were immediately supplied to the best German squadrons, including von Richthofen's Jagdgeschwader Nr. 1. After the surrender, Anthony Fokker managed to smuggle D 7 engines and parts to Holland, where, after having been assembled, they formed the backbone of the Dutch air force. (National Air and Space Museum, Washington, D.C.)

Guaranteed to give a hot time to any Allied airman who
makes a low pass over this "German" aerodrome.
(Rhinebeck Aerodrome, Rhinebeck, N.Y.)

58

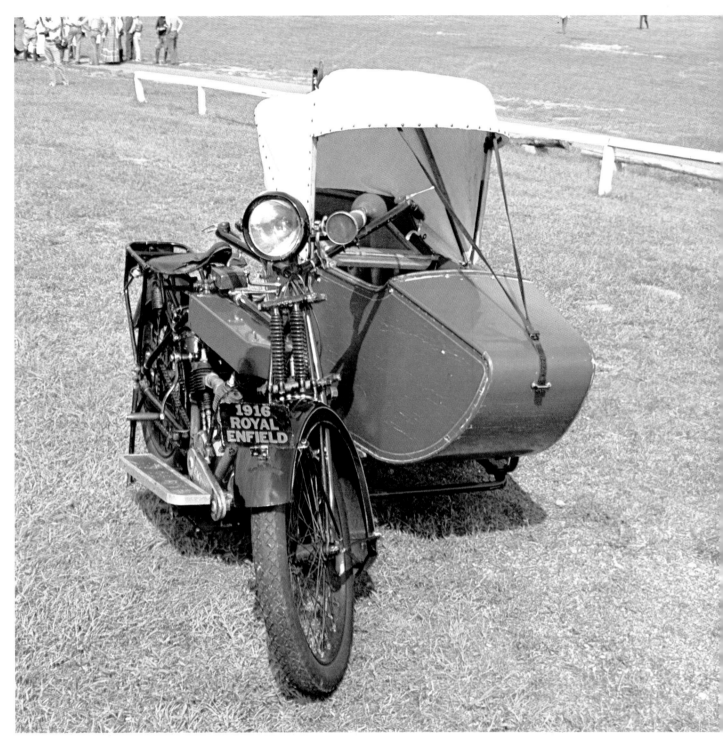

Sir "Boom," your conveyance awaits! (Rhinebeck
Aerodrome, Rhinebeck, N.Y.)

A total of eighty Siemens-Schukert D 3s saw action in 1918. Their outstanding characteristics were excellent maneuverability and rate of climb. (Rhinebeck Aerodrome, Rhinebeck, N.Y.)

A Nieuport 28 and a Fokker Dr. 1 side by side—French gracefulness and German ruggedness. That's how their builder, Jim Appleby, describes them. (Flabob Airport, Riverside, Calif.)

The fuselage frame of a Curtiss Jenny. Now you know why they were called "crates." (Cradle of Aviation Museum, Mineola, N.Y.)

War-surplus Standard J-1 biplanes shared with the Jenny
the distinction of being the mainstays of the barnstorming
and air circus circuits. (Movieland of the Air Museum,
Orange County Airport, Calif.)

The Douglas M-2 biplane used by the U.S. Air Mail Service in 1926 was a vast improvement over its war-surplus De Havillands. (National Air and Space Museum, Washington, D.C.)

In 1928, the feisty little Pitcairn Mailwing flew the New York–Atlanta run in just seven hours—one-third of the time it took by rail. (Rhinebeck Aerodrome, Rhinebeck, N.Y.)

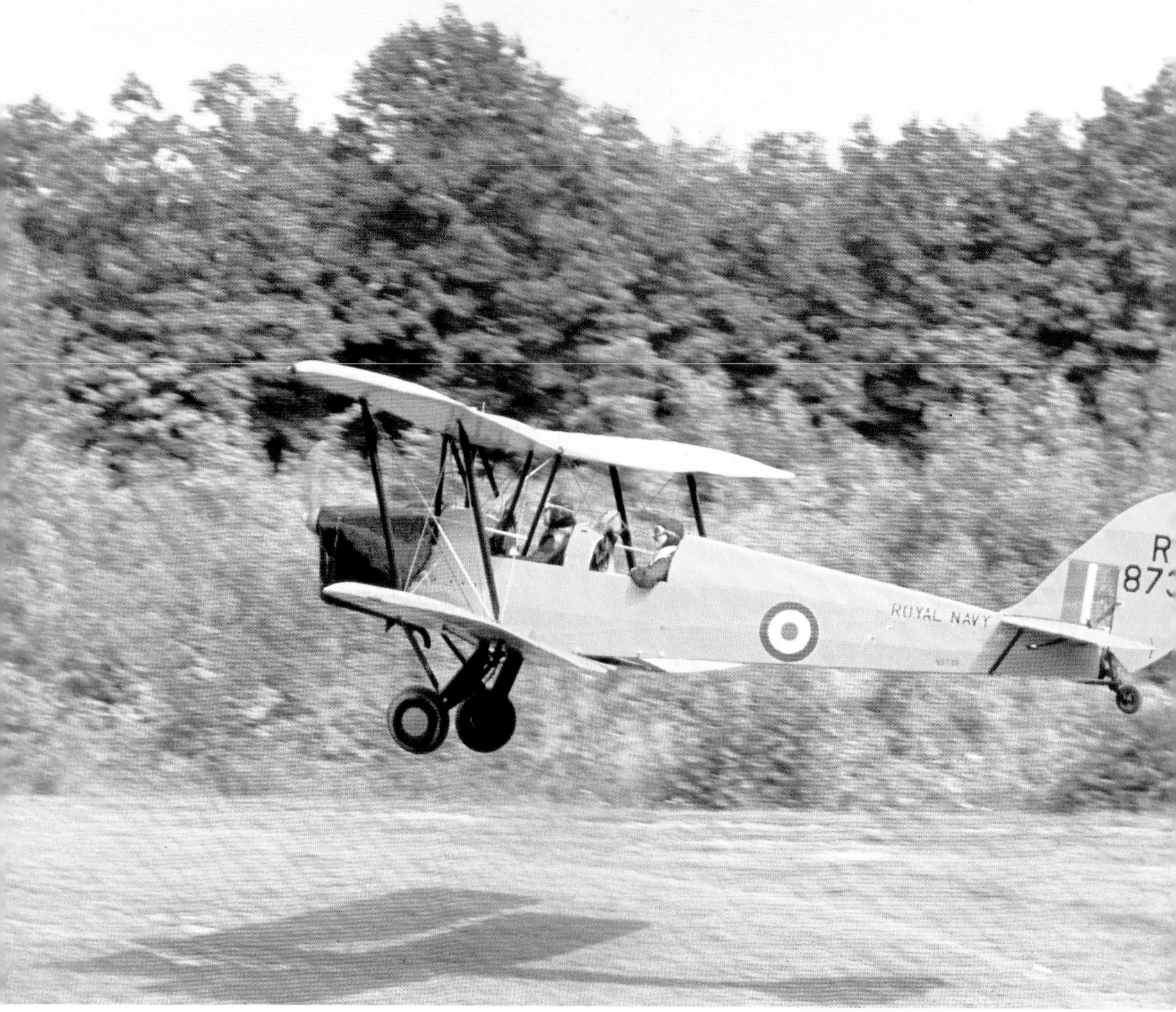
ROYAL NAVY

The delightfully foursquare-looking plane seen landing here is a De Havilland Tiger Moth. From 1931 through 1945 large numbers of them were built. They were used by the RAF (Royal Air Force) as trainers through World War II and were a favorite of flying clubs and private owners throughout the British Empire. (Rhinebeck Aerodrome, Rhinebeck, N.Y.)

The dual-control cockpits of the Tiger Moth. (Rhinebeck
Aerodrome, Rhinebeck, N.Y.)

Is it a wingless plane? No, it's the gondola of the good blimp *Pilgrim*. The first airship to be inflated with helium, the *Pilgrim* had room for two passengers who could relax in the luxury of mohair velour upholstered seats framed in mahogany veneer, all the while enjoying the view, as they cruised at a leisurely forty mph. The *Pilgrim* made its first flight on June 3, 1925, and was retired on December 30, 1931, having carried 5,355 passengers a total of 94,974 miles over a period of 2,880 hours in the air. (National Air and Space Museum, Washington, D.C.)

The 1929 Curtiss Fledgling is a civilian version of the U.S.
Navy NC2-1 trainer. Slow and steady, it was a bit
old-fashioned, even in its day. Of the approximately 100
that were built, some were used in South American
branches of Curtiss flight schools and a few in Hollywood
grade B war pictures. (Rhinebeck Aerodrome,
Rhinebeck, N.Y.)

Its nose looking, for all the world, like a face sporting a "shiner," the Great Lakes 2T1E of 1931 was the leading American aerobatic plane for two decades. (Rhinebeck Aerodrome, Rhinebeck, N.Y.)

The story behind this particular plane is indeed
fascinating. Built in 1928 as a standard model PA-5
Pitcairn Mailwing, it was Harold Pitcairn's personal plane.
In 1930 he returned it to his factory for modification,
adding the wings and tail surfaces of a later model, the
PA-7. In 1977 his son, Steve Pitcairn, a former airlines
pilot for Eastern Airlines, bought it from a museum, not
realizing at the time of purchase that it had been his
father's plane. (Robinsville Airport, Robinsville, N.J.)

The star performer of the Great American Flying Circus,
a 1929 Travelair 4000, kept in mint condition by its owner,
John Talmadge. (Brookhaven Airport, Brookhaven, N.Y.)

The 1930 Lockheed Vega, *Winnie Mae*, won fame for both itself and its pilot, Wiley Post, when it set a number of world records. The first was the National Air Races, when it set a record flying from Los Angeles to Chicago in nine hours, nine minutes, and four seconds on August 27, 1930. With Harold Gatty as his navigator, on June 23, 1931, Post took off in the *Winnie Mae* from New York on a world-circling flight that was to set another record: eight days, fifteen hours, and fifty-one minutes. Two years later the *Winnie Mae*, equipped with the recently developed radio compass and autopilot, was flown solo by Wiley Post on another around-the-world flight. Leaving New York on July 15, 1933, he arrived back in that city, having circled the globe in seven days, eighteen hours, and forty-nine minutes. (National Air and Space Museum, Washington, D.C.)

One spiffy-looking bird, the Stout Sky Car was designed and built by William B. Stout of Ford Trimotor fame in 1931. Its corrugated aluminum body, built around a tubular-steel fuselage frame, followed contemporary automobile design. It was intended to be a simple, safe, and comfortable personal plane, and it was. Unfortunately, the model shown here was the only one to get off the ground. (Silver Hill Museum, Silver Hill, Md.)

This most improbable-looking craft, which looks as though
it came straight out of a Jules Verne novel, is actually
the 1933 brainchild of another Frenchman, Henri Mignet.
"Le Pou de ciel" ("Sky Flea") was intended to be the
ultimate do-it-yourself airplane. It could be built for $350
and, according to its inventor, was so simple to operate
that anyone could teach himself to fly. The Pou de ciel
craze swept throughout Europe for a time, but its alarming
accident rate finally ended its short day of glory. (Silver
Hill Museum, Silver Hill, Md.)

This beautiful Fairchild 24-W sports plane, of around 1934, stands, like a ghostly image out of some glamorous past, all by itself in a cavernous darkened hangar. (Long Beach Airport, Long Beach, Calif.)

The Northrop 2B-Gamma, *Polar Star*, 1933. In 1935
explorer Lincoln Ellsworth and pilot Herbert
Hollick-Kenyon took off from Dundee Island in the
Weddell Sea on a flight across Antarctica that was intended
to end in Little America. A dwindling fuel supply forced
them to make a hard landing at the Bay of Whales, which
accounts for the dent in the fuselage directly behind the
engine. They walked for six days in order to complete the
trip. Hollick-Kenyon later returned to reclaim the plane.
(Silver Hill Museum, Silver Hill, Md.)

Ole Miss', a Curtiss Robin dating from 1928. Using
air-to-air refueling, Fred and Algene Key kept this plane
in the sky for twenty-seven days, a world record for
sustained flight. (Silver Hill Museum, Silver Hill, Md.)

The Grumman JTF-6 Duck first made its appearance in 1935. Odd though it may look, it served the Navy, the Marine Corps, and the Coast Guard in admirable fashion, assuming duties ranging from target towing to air-sea rescue missions. Ducks are still flying in remote places. (Movieland of the Air Museum, Orange County Airport, Calif.)

Winged Art Deco: Steve Pitcairn's 1935 Waco CUC-2
cabin biplane. (Robinsville Airport, Robinsville, N.J.)

The engine cowling of the Waco CUC-2, one of the
greatest looking ever. (Robinsville Airport,
Robinsville, N.J.)

John Turgian, a U.S. Air captain, not only rescued his
1936 Spartan Model 7-W Executive from oblivion he
restored it to its original opulence, which makes it nothing
less than a flying Rolls-Royce limousine. (Robinsville
Airport, Robinsville, N.J.)

When the Douglas DC-3 was introduced in 1936, it put
commercial aviation in the really big time once and for all.
According to C. R. Smith, president at the time of
American Airlines, "It was the first airplane in the world
that could make money just by hauling passengers."
It wasn't long before every major airline in the world was
flying DC-3s. During World War II it performed yeoman
service as a troop transport and freight carrier for every
Allied power, including the Russians who, under license,
made a version of their own. (Long Beach Airport,
Long Beach, Calif.)

Grace the Ace, a lady in her fifties, established the world's spin record of eighty turns on February 8, 1978, at Tucson, Arizona, in this antique Piper J-3 Cub. The somewhat disheveled right wing is the result of a stunt: flying at an angle and scraping the runway. (Mojave Airport, Mojave, Calif.)

The Lockheed Lodestar, introduced as a medium transport plane in 1938, also joined the colors, the first being those of the RAF in 1939. (Long Beach Airport, Long Beach, Calif.)

Here is a beautiful example of what is perhaps the world's most famous aerobatic plane, the Pitts Special, first built in 1943 by Curtiss Pitts. Then, in the early 1960s, he offered plans for $125. Now there are around 250 of them, like this model S-1C, flying; most of them built in backyards, home workshops, and garages. (Mojave Airport, Mojave, Calif.)

A great favorite of antique airplane buffs: the
fabulous-looking Stearman trainer of World War II fame.
(Brookhaven Airport, Brookhaven, N.Y.)

BIBLIOGRAPHY

Angelucci, Enzo, and Matricardi, Paolo. *World Aircraft: Origins–World War I*. Chicago: Rand McNally & Co., 1979.

Glines, Carroll V., Jr. *The Compact History of the United States Air Force*. rev. ed. New York: Hawthorn Books, 1973.

Munson, Kenneth. *Bombers, Patrol and Reconnaissance Aircraft 1914–1919*. New York: The Macmillan Company, 1968.

Oakes, Claudia, comp. *Aircraft of the National Air and Space Museum*. Washington, D.C.: Smithsonian Institution, 1976.

Penrose, Harald. *British Aviation: The Pioneer Years 1903–1914*. Fallbrook, Calif.: Aero Publishers, 1967.

Rickenbacker, Edward. *Fighting the Flying Circus*. Edited and with a foreword by Arch Whitehouse. Garden City, N.Y.: Doubleday & Co., 1965.

Tallman, Frank. *Flying the Old Planes*. Preface by Ernest K. Gann; introduction by Joe Brown. Garden City, N.Y.: Doubleday & Co., 1973.

Ulanoff, Stanley. *Illustrated History of World War I in the Air*. New York: Arco Publishing, 1975.

Vecsey, George, and Dade, George C. *Getting Off the Ground*. New York: E. P. Dutton, 1979.

Whitehouse, Arch. *The Years of the Sky Kings*. Garden City, N.Y.: Doubleday & Co., 1959.

JOHN HALPERN was born in New York City and attended Dartmouth College. He has been a television director at two major advertising agencies. Mr. Halpern then worked on documentary films for the Massachusetts Institute of Technology and Time-Life, Inc., which were shown on television and in classrooms. Because he had always been interested in architecture, he proposed and has been working on an ongoing project for the Avery Library of Columbia University called "The Changing Face of America," which documents architecture photographically, both past and present, from New England, the Middle Atlantic States, and California. He is the author of *New York/New York* (1978) and *Los Angeles: Improbable City* (1979).